The People who lived in Hanley in 1864

Compiled by Geoffrey Lindop

MERCIANOTES

Cover Picture:

Market Square, Hanley
Circa 1900
From a picture postcard

Notes on the entries

^x an asterisk denotes no address cited. In the original directory the word 'colour' was spelt 'color'. The words 'Shakespeare Buildings' were spelt 'Shakspere Buildings'.

First published 2011
Revised and enlarged 2014

Published by:
Mercianotes
Wigton
CA7 5AQ
United Kingdom

© 2011 Mercianotes

ISBN (10) :1501043226
ISBN (13) :9781501043222

The People who lived in Hanley in 1864

Parish	Miles from Hanley	Direction
Bucknall-cum-Bagnall	1.2	East
Burslem	1.4	North by North West
Stoke-upon-Trent	1.4	South by South West
Newcastle under Lyme	2	West by South West
Wolstanton	2	West by North West
Bradeley	2.5	North
Norton-in-the-Moors	2.6	North by North East
Longton	2.8	South by South East
Blurton	3.2	South by South East
Trentham	3.8	South
Newchapel	4.5	North by North West
Endon	4.5	North by North East
Keele	5.1	West by South West
Caverswall	5.3	South East
Barlaston	5.6	South
Audley	5.9	West by North West
Dilhorne	6.1	East by South East
Whitmore	6.1	South West
Biddulph	6.2	North
Cheddleton	6.4	East by North East
Church Lawton	6.6	North West
Chorlton	6.6	South West
Madeley	7.1	West by South West
Horton	7.2	North by North East
Alsager	7.5	North West
Creswell	7.5	South East
Kingsley	7.5	East
Fulford	7.6	South East
Draycott-in-the-Moors	7.6	South East
Swynnerton	7.7	South by South West
Odd Rode	7.9	North West
Maer	7.9	South West

Private Residents.

Abington, Leonard James, esq. High st
Adams, Mr. Charles, Charles street
Allbut, Mr. Edwin, Howard place
Alkins, Charles, esq. Bromfield house
Amos, Samuel, esq. Albion street
Ash, Mr. George, Havelock place
Ashworth, Taylor, esq. Cleveland house
Askey, Mr. John, Mollart street

Baguley, Mr George, Snowhill
Baddeley, Misses, Northwood
Baddeley, Richard Mumford, esq.
        Northwood
Baker, Edward, esq. Porthill
Baker, John, esq. The Hollys, Northwood
Banks, Mr. Edward, Havelock place
Barlow, Mr. Joseph, Prospect terrace
Beaumont, Mr. George, Wellington st
Blakiston, Matthew Folliott, esq.
        Shelton lodge
Blower, Mrs. Broad street
Boothroyd, Benjamin, esq. Market street
Brandon, Mr. Wm. Philip, Howard place
Brook, Mr. William, Harley street
Brown, Hugh, esq. Albion street
Brownfield, Mr. Job, Albion street
Brownfield, Wm. esq. J.P. Chatterley ho
Brown, Westhead Thomas Chappell,
        esq. Cauldon place

Campbell, Mrs. Broad street, Piccadilly
Caslon, Mr. William, Bucknall road
Challinor, Edward, esq. Pall mall
Chetwynd, Mr. Elijah, Howard place

Chetwynd, Mrs. Havelock place
Clarke, Mr. Richard, Havelock place
Clementmon, Sir. Joseph, Howard place
Cope, Mr. William S.
        The Cottage, Northwood
Cox, Mrs. Wheatley cottage.
Crowe, Rev. John [Presbyterian],
        Windsor street
Cunningham, Thomas, esq. Market sq

Davis, Francis, esq. The Cottage, Well st
Davis, Joseph Barnard, M.D. Albion st
Davis, William Haslam, esq. Lamb street
Dimmock, John, esq. Lichfield street
Dimont, Rev. James [curate of St. Luke's],
        Nelson place
Dix, Alexander Mills, esq. Grove house
Dodd, Mrs. Spring vllla, Northwood

Eastwood, Rev. Jonathan, M.A.
        Parsonage, Lichfield street

Fairmann, John Bertram,. esq. Broad st
Fisher, Mrs. Northwood
Folker, Wm. Henry, esq. Market street
Forbes, James, esq. Caledonia house
Forbes, Joseph Samual esq. Crescent villa
Ford, Mr. Thomas, Richmond villa
Foster, Mr. Henry, Albion street

Garner, Robert, esq. Winton villa
Gerrard Mrs. Spring villa, Northwood
Gibbs, Mrs. Stafford street

Gilbert, Mr. John, Market street
Girdlestone, Horatio, esq. Albion street
Grant, Rev. Francis Bazett,M.A. Rectory
Grosvenor, William, esq. Old Hall street

Hammersley, Miss, Havelock place
Harding, Joseph B. esq. East View pl
Harding, Mr. William, Mollart street
Harrington, Mr. James, Broad street
Hassell, Mr. William, Pall mall
Hawley, Mr. William, Cauldon place
Hoare, Rev. Francis, B.A. Broad street
Homer, Mr. Charles James H.
        The Fenns house, Stockton
        brook
Hulme, Mr. John, Snow hill

Irwin, Mrs. Snow hill

Jackson, Rev. Charles Bird, M.A.
        [incumbent], Northwood
Johnson, Mrs. Vine street
Jones, Rev. Edward Hugh [curate],
        Bucknall road

Keeling, Mr. John, Bagnall street
Keeling, Samuel, esq. Eastwood house
Keeling, Thomas, esq. (mayor of
        Hanley), Howard place

Livesey, William, esq. Charles street
Lloyd, Mrs. Broom street
Lockett, Charles, esq. Howard place
Luscombe, Henry, esq. Russell street

McBean, Alexander, esq. New street
Marks, Mr. Edwin, Far Green cottage
Marsden, Rev. Henry [New Connexion],
        Broom street
Martin, William, esq. Cauldon place
Meakin, George, esq. Northwood
Moore, Geo. Lennox, esq. Shelton
        house
Moore, William, esq. Richmond terrace
Mountford, John, esq. New Park villa
Moxon, James, esq. Brunswick street

Narramore, Mr. Robert Edwin, King st

Ogden Miss, New street

Paddock, George, esq. Grove House
Paddock George, jun. esq. Grove house
Palmer Mr. Frederick, Church street
Palmer William, esq
Palmer William Turner, esq. Church st
Pankhurst Mr. James Wm. Mollart street
Peake Mr. John Machin Sun Hill house
Perry Mr. Hugh B. Park street
Phillips Mr. Edward, Bagnall street
Pidduck Mr. Henry, Havelock place
Potter Mr. Thomas Andrew, Mollart st
Powell Edward, esq. Charles street

Ridgway Edward John, esq. J.P.
Ridgway Mrs. Cauldon place
Ridgway Mr. William, Northwood
Roden William S. esq. Etruria hall
Rowley Mrs. Broad street

Sale Mrs. Wellington street
Salt Mr. Samuel, Russell street
Scott Henry, esq. Albion street
Scrivener Robert, esq. Howard place
Shelley Miss, Havelock. place
Shirley Mr. John, Market street
Smith Rev. Richard Henry, Lichfield st
Smith Charles J. esq. Northwood
Stevenson Ralph, esq. Bagnall street

Taylor Mr. Edward, Prospect terrace
Taylor Mr. James, Broad street
Taylor William, esq. Park villa
Taylor Mr. William, Providence square
Tennant Edmund, esq. Wheatley
        cottage, Bucknall road

Vigers Mr. Thomas, Russell street

Walker James G. esq. Market square

Walker Mr. John Swift, Old Hall terrace
Ward Henry, esq. Albion house
Ward Henry, jun. esq. Albion house
Wardle Mr. James, Havelock place
Whidborne Rev. George Ferris, M.A.
 Parsonage, Old Hall street
Whittingham John Fowler, esq. Albion st
Wilkins Rev. Nathaniel George [curate],
 Spring villa, Northwood

Williamson Mr Samuel, Plough street
Worrillow Mrs. Mollart street
Worsfold Rev. John Napper, Wellington
 parsonage, Lichfield street
Worthington Mr. Thomas, Mollart st

Yates Miss, Snow hill
Yates Mr. Horton, Howard place

Hanley in 1864

HANLEY is a rapidly increasing and improving borough and market town, the most populous of the pottery towns, pleasantly situated in;

- North Pirehill hundred,
- the parish Stoke-upon-Trent;
- parliamentary borough of Stoke-upon-Trent,
- deanery of Stoke-upon-Trent,
- archdeaconry of Stafford,
- and diocese of Lichfield.

The streets are wide and well paved, and the town is well supplied with water and gas.

In the year 1857 the townships of Hanley and Shelton were incorporated, and constitute the municipal borough of Hanley, John. Ridgway, of Cauldon-place, being the first mayor. All, local authority was vested in the corporation except the market trust, which still continued an independent body, holding property, tollages etc., under lease from: the lord of the manor, until the year 1862, when that also was transferred to the town council.

Northwood, Eastwood Vale, Mount Pleasant and Etruria are suburbs belonging to the town. The population in 1861 was 33,009 (Shelton, 18,331; Hanley,14,678), and has since considerably increased. Shelton was the birthplace of Fenton the poet, in 1683; the house is still standing, though in a very dilapidated state.

Continued on page 4

From page 3

Hanley church (St. John the Evangelist) was founded in 1737, and rebuilt in 1788. The present structure is a brick edifice, with a square tower containing eight bells, and affords rather more than 1,250 sittings, which at that time was thought sufficient church accommodation for the population. The oldest existing register bears date in 1789, the registration books having been partly destroyed by the mob in the Chartist riots in 1842. The living is a perpetual curacy, in the gift of twenty-six trustees, value about £300 per annum, with residence. The first incumbent, the Rev. J. Middleton, held the living for sixty-two years, and the second, the Rev. R. E. Aitken, forty-seven, making up this extraordinary amount of nearly 110 years between them. The present incumbent, the Rev. G. F. Whidborne, A.M., of Queen's College, Oxford, was instituted in 1849.

Shelton church (St. Mark) is a large and elegant Gothic stone edifice, with a tower 120 feet high, erected. in 1834, at a cost of £11,000, and affords accommodation for 2,000 persons. The eastern window has a rare specimen of stained glass. The living is a rectory, in the gift of Wilberforce Heelas, Esq., value about £520 per annum, held by the Rev. F. B. Grant, M.A. of Christ Church, Oxford, who has a neat stone rectory-house on a small portion of glebe land.

There are also, four district parish churches; Etruria, Northwood, Hope and Wellington that were built under what is commonly called Sir Robert Peel's Act. in the gift of the Crown and bishop alternately, and each endowed with £150 per annum, with a residence, besides pew rents and surplice fees, *viz*:

Etruria church (St. Matthew's), consecrated 1849, and containing 723 sittings, Rev. C. J. Sterling; A.R., St. Mary Hall, Oxford, incumbent;

Northwood church (Holy Trinity), consecrated 1849, Rev. C. B. Jackson, A.M., Brasenose College, Oxford, incumbent;

Hope church (Trinity), consecrated 1848, and containing 650 sittings, Rev. Jonathan Eastwood, A.M., St. John's College, Cambridge, incumbent.

Wellington church (St. Luke's), consecrated 1854, and containing 800 sittings, Revs J. N.Worsfold, incumbent.

Continued on page 26

Commercial

Acres, Thomas P., *linendraper*, Market square

Adams, Boyce, *grocer*, Piccadilly

Adams, Charlotte (Mrs.), *milliner*, Broad street

Adams, Henry, *printer*, Hope street

Adams, Thomas, *hop & malt merchant*, Church street

Adams see Keeling & Adams

Adney, William, *colour maker*, Shelton wharf

Akers, Edward, *tailor*, Northwood

Aldersea, Sarah (Mrs.), *confectioner*, High Street

Alfieri, Charles, *boarding school*, Northwood

Allbut & Daniel, *booksellers*, Tontine sq.

Allcock, Ralph, *saddler*, Stafford street

Alldridge, Charles, *confectioner*, Piccadilly

Allen, Ann (Mrs.), *confectioner*, Parliament row

Allen, Herbert George, *china manufacturer*, Broad street

Allen, John, *shopkeeper*, Mollart street

Allen, Lenford, *butcher*, Parliament row

Allen, Thomas, *artist*, Howard place

Allsop, Josiah, *butcher*, Bucknall road

Amos, Samuel, *solicitor, & high bailiff to county court*, Albion street

Anderson, William, *innkeeper*, Grapes, Tontine passage

Anderton Company *Duke of Bridgewater's Trustees*, Etrurian Vale wharf

Andrew, Mary (Mrs.), *straw bonnet maker*, Bryan street

Arkley, Mary (Mrs.), *beer retailer*, High street

Ash see Wardle & Ash

Ashworth, George L. & Brothers (late Morley & Ashworth), *ironstone china & earthenware manufacturers, & sole makers of Mason's patent ironstone china, patterns & shapes*, Broad street

Austin, Harriet (Mrs.), *shopkeeper*, Marsh street

Austin, Joseph, *bricklayer*, Joiner's square

Averill, Thomas, *confectioner*, Broad street

Baddeley, James, *rustic ware maker*, Gloucester street and John street

Baddeley, Richard, *colliery owner*, Northwood

Baddeley, Wm. Warburton, *veterinary surgeon*, Lichfield street

Bagnall, John, *shopkeeper*, Trinity street

Baguley, George, *china manufacturer**

Bailey Murrells & Co. *majolica, parian etc. Manufacturers,* Elm street

Bailey, John, *beer retailer,* New street

Baines, Charles, *secretary,* Staffordshire Potteries Waterworks Co., Albion street

Baker, John & George, *wholesale & retail wine & spirit merchants;* and at Burslem

Baker, John, *grocer,* Parliament row

Ball, Thomas, *beer retailer,* Northwood

Barcroft, Charles, *basket maker,* Market square

Barcroft, John, *basket maker,* Parliament row

Barcroft, Susan (Mrs.), *milliner,* Parliament row

Barker, Elizabeth (Mrs.), *greengrocer,* Hope street

Barker, William, *hosier,* Hope street

Barlow, James, *shopkeeper,* Mount Pleasant

Barlow, Rebecca (Mrs.), *beer retailer,* Stafford street

Barlow, William Henry, *innkeeper,* Marquis of Granby, Stafford st

Barrett, David, *beer retailer,* Vale place

Barrett, William, *tailor,* Hope street

Barrow, John, *boiler maker,* Bucknall rd

Bartholomew, Sarah (Mrs.), *beer retailer,* Market square

Bate, James, *beer retailer,* Hill street

Bates, Cornelius, *boot & shoe maker,* Bucknall road

Bates, Joseph, *hairdresser,* Hope street

Bates, William, *nail maker,* Trinity street

Beardmore, Theophilus, *innkeeper,* New Market Tavern, Tontine st.

Bebbington, James, *bookseller & stationer,* Broad street

Beddall, John, *mattress maker,* Miles bank

Beddow, Martha & Eleanor (Misses), *shopkeepers,* Sun street

Beddow, Emma (Miss), *milliner,* Marsh street

Bednall, Joseph, *tailor,* Clarence street

Beech, George, *beer retailer,* Hope st

Beech, Henry, *hairdresser,* Broad street

Beech, Mary (Mrs.), *shopkeeper,* Etruria road

Beech, Robert, *saddler,* Parliament row

Beech, William, *baker,* Old Hall street

Beeteson, Edne (Mrs.), *bootmaker,* Piccadilly

Belfield, Ann (Mrs.), *beer retailer,* Etruria road.

Bell, John, *tailor,* Piccadilly

Benjamin Solomon & Co., *clothiers,* Market square

Bentley, Elizabeth (Mrs.), *dressmaker,* Harley street

Bentley, Marinda (Mrs.), *shopkeeper,* Nelson place

Berks, Charles, *hairdresser,* High street

Berks, Henry, *confectioner,* Piccadilly

Berks, William, *grocer*

Berrisford, Benjamin, *trunk maker,* New Hall street

Berrisford, George, *tailor,* Broad street

Berrisford, Henry, *blacksmith,* High street

Berrisford, John, shopkeeper, Albert place

Berry, William, *innkeeper,* Golden Lion, Market square

Bevington, John, *manufacturer of china, majolica, ornamental parian, earthenware etc.,* Great York st. & Clarence st.

Bevington, Samuel, *manufacturer of porcelain, parian statuettes & earthenware,* Brunswick street & Marsh street

Bickerton, Thomas, *baker,* Great York st.

Bickley - *see Scarratt & Bickley*

Biddulph, William, *innkeeper,* Windmill, Hill street

Billington, James, *plumber,* Old Hall street

Billington, Richard, *hairdresser,* Miles bank

Binns, George, *wholesale clog & pattern manufacturer,* Piccadilly

Birch, Elijah & Co.
> *dealers in glazed stoneware,*
> *sewerage pipes, terra cotta*
> *chimney tops & pots, fire bricks,*
> *blueware, plaster of paris,*
> *cement etc.,*
> Broad street

Birch, Charles, *innkeeper*, Ship,
> Providence square

Birchall, Robert, *plumber*, Bryan street

Birkin, Bryan, *shopkeeper*, Etruria road

Bishop & Blakiston *solicitors*,
> Howard place

Bishop, James, *baker*, Crown bank

Bladun, Edward, *beer retailer*, Marsh st

Blagg, Henry, *innkeeper*, Angel, High
> street

Blakeley, William, *boot & shoe maker*,
> Market square

Blakeman, Henry, *beer retailer*, Hope st

Blakiston see Bishop & Blakiston

Bloor, Francis Elijah, *beer retailer*,
> Trinity st.

Blundell, Catherine (Mrs.),
> *fancy repository*, Lamb street

Boddington, William C.,
> *potters' material dealer*, Snow
> hill

Boden, John, *innkeeper*, Cat inn,
> Northwood

Bodley, Edward Fisher,
> *commercial traveller*,
> Howard place

Boon, Edward, *beer retailer*, Windmill st

Boone, Alfred, *colour manufacturer*,
> Old Hall terrace

Booth, George, *auctioneer*. George st

Booth, Richard, *chemist & druggist*,
> Parliament row

Booth, Thomas,
> *britannia metal manufacturer*,
> Lichfield street

Booth, William Ward,
> *manufacturing chemist*,
> Parker street

Boothroyd, Benjamin, *surgeon*, Market
> street

Boothroyd, Emmerson, *joiner*,
> Brunswick street

Boston, John, *boot & shoe maker*,
> Tontine square

Boughey, William, *shopkeeper*, Broom
> street

Boult, Charles, *tailor*, Broad street

Boulton, John & Son, *linendrapers*, Lamb
> street

Boulton, Charles Bourne,
> *general dealer*, Lamb street

Boulton, Eliza (Mrs.), *shopkeeper*,
> Hope street

Boulton, John, *beer retailer*, Mollart st

Bourne, Samuel, *linendraper*, Hope st

Bowers, William, *flint grinder*,
> Joiner's square

Boyd, John, *hatter*, Broad street

Bradbury, Samuel, *fishmonger*,
> Broad street

Bradbury, Thomas, *brickmaker*,
> Eastwood vale

Bradbury, Thomas, *greengrocer*,
> Eastwood vale

Bradbury, William, *grocer & provision*
> *dealer*, Well street

Bradford, George, *linendraper*, High st

Bradley, Joseph, *watch & clock maker*,
> New Hall street

Bradshaw, John,
> *merchant, exporter of china &*
> *earthenware & lamps, &*
> *importer of marbles & wines,*
> Havelock place

Brammer, Ann (Mrs.), *general dealer*,
> Broad street

Brassington, Edward Henry, *Secretary*,
> Staffordshire Potteries Street
> Railway Co.

Breveton, John, *clothier*, Stafford street

Brierley, Mary (Mrs.), *innkeeper*, Sea
> Lion, High street

Brierley see Crapper & Brierley,

Brindley, Lucy (Mrs.), *shopkeeper*, Sun
> street

British Gas Light Co. Ltd.
> (John Haswell, manager),
> offices, Pall mall

Brittain, Thomas & Son, *paper makers*,
> Bucknall road

Broadhurst, James & George, *grocers,*
Broad street
Brock, William, *china dealer,* Piccadilly
Brockley, George, *marine store dealer,*
Miles bank
Brook, John, *butcher,* Northwood
Brooks, Ralph, *wheelwright,* High street
Brooksby, Agnes (Mrs.), *milliner,* Hill st
Brooksby, Henry, *tailor,* Hill street
Broom, Elizabeth (Mrs.),
boot & shoe maker, Trinity
street
Broster, Ann (Mrs.), *provision dealer,*
Bryan street
Brough, Ann (Mrs.), *milliner,* Windsor
street
Brougham, William, *tinplate worker,*
William street
Broughton, Samuel, *leatherseller,*
High street
Brown, George, *chemist,* Bryan street
Brown, Hugh, *solicitor, &*
vice-consul for America,
Albion street
Brown, James, *shopkeeper,* Russell st
Brown, John, *chemist,* Market square
Brown, Samuel, *tobacconist,* Hope st
Brown, Thomas, *grocer,* Sun street
Brown *see Till & Brown*
Browne, Samuel, *milliner,* Hope street
Brownfield, William, *flint grinder,*
New Hall mill
Brown Westhead (T. C.), Moore & Co.,
china, earthenware, porcelain
statuary & sanitary vessel
manufacturers & stoneware of
every description used by
druggists,
Cauldun place; etc.
107 Hatton garden, London EC
Brunt, E, see Pottery Mechanics'
Institution
Brunt, Jeremiah, *greengrocer,* Hope st
Bryant, William, *bricklayer,* Broad street
Buck, Ann (Mrs.), *dining rooms,*
Piccadilly
Buckley, James, *tailor,* Hope street
Buckley, John, *manufacturer of superior*
glazed water closet pans &
traps, angular urinals & every
description of sanitary ware,
beer machine handle maker &
decorator,
Vine Street works
Buckley, John, *miller,* Marsh street
Bull, John, *butcher,* Hope street
Bull, Joseph, *ironworks,* Cliff vale
Buller (Wentworth William) & Mugford,
patent cock spur & still
manufacturers
(Charles A. Draycott, manager),
works, Joiner's square
Burn, William & Co. *clay merchants,*
St. Austell
(John Hollins, sole agent),
Northwood
Burndred, James, *blacksmith,* Marsh st
Burton, Joseph, *butcher,* Tontine street
Butters, Charles, *pawnbroker,*
Marsh street
Butterworth, John,
market superintendent & agent
to the Liverpool & London
assurance company,
King street
Buxton, Ann (Mrs.), *hosier,* Lamb street

Cade, William, *hatter,* Tontine square
Cadman, M. A. (Miss),
milliner & dressmaker,
Miles bank
Capewell, Edward, *shopkeeper,* Lichfield
street
Capper, Joseph, *wheelwright,* Lichfield st
Carpmail, Moses, *beer retailer &*
butcher, Sun street
Carr, George, *boot & shoe maker,* Elm st
Carr, Hannah (Mrs.), *hosier,* Hope street
Carr, Peter, *innkeeper,* Queen's Head,
Bryan street
Cartledge, Henry,
secretary to the Staffordshire
Potteries loan society,
Miles bank
Cartlidge, George, *hatter,* Hope street
Cartlidge, Joseph, *boot & shoe maker,*
Parker street

Cartlidge, Theophilus,
    nursery & seedsman,
    Finney gardens, Bucknall road

Cartwright, Ann (Miss), *milliner,* Harley
    street

Castellow, Michael, *shopkeeper,* Marsh
    street

Challinor, Edward, *solicitor,*
    registrar to county court,
    town clerk, clerk to burial
    board & to local board,
    Cheapside

Challinor, Samuel, *beer retailer,*
    Piccadilly

Chantrey, Thomas, *professor of music,*
    Tontine passage

Charlesworth, Richard, *clogger,* High st.

Charlesworth, Richard, *shopkeeper,*
    Cauldon place

Charlesworth, William, *beer retailer,*
    Hope street

Cheadle, Joseph Chesworth, *innkeeper,*
    Clough inn, Tinker's dough

Cherry, John Law, *reporter,* King street

Cherry, Joseph, *beer retailer,*
    Joiner's square

Chester, Stephen, *photographic artist,*
    Piccadilly

Chetwin, Joseph, *boot & shoe maker,*
    Cleveland passage

Chetwynd Brothers,
    modellers & designers,
    Havelock place

Chowner, John, *butcher,* Bryan street

Clark, George, *muffin baker,* Hope street

Clarke, William, *boot & shoe maker,*
    Russell street

Clay, William & Co., *flint grinders,*
    Nelson place

Clarke see Holmes & Clarke

Clementson, James,
    earthenware manufacturer,
    Broad street

Clewes, Jesse, *stonemason,*
    Lichfield street

Clewes, William, jun., *innkeeper,*
    Cheshire Cheese, Chell street

Clewlow, Sarah (Mrs.), *dressmaker,*
    Bryan street

Cliff, Robert, *beer retailer,* Swan passage

Clifford & Griffiths, *linendrapers,*
    silk mercers, hosiers,
    haberdashers & undertakers,
    Lamb street

Coates & Co., *silk lawn manufacturers,*
    Marsh street

Colclough, Benjamin, *beer retailer,*
    Bryan street

Colclough, Elizabeth (Mrs.), *beer retailer,*
    Regent street

Colclough, Hannah (Miss), *milliner,*
    Broad street

Colclough, Isaac, *innkeer,* Railway inn,
    Providence square

Colclough, John, *innkeer,* Rising Sun,
    Broad street

Colclough, Samuel, *carpenter,* Charles
    street

Cole, Samuel & Co., *glass dealers,*
    Piccadilly & Norfolk street

Cole, Samuel, *superintendent of police,*
    Market square

Collett, Bernard, *grocer,* Market square

Collison, Thomas.,
    general commission agent,
    Parker. street & Tunstall

Conway, Edward, *shopkeeper,* Bath
    street

Cooke see Hill & Cooke

Cooper, Ellen (Miss), *beer retailer,*
    Bucknall road

Cooper, Francis, *coach builder, & all*
    kinds of carriages made &
    repaired, Bryan street

Cooper, John, *grocer,* New street

Cooper, Thomas, *china manufacturer*

Cooper, William, *shopkeeper,* Hope
    street

Cope, Thomas, *boot & shoe maker,*
    Northwood

Cope, Thomas, *provision dealer,* Broad
    street

Copeland, Benjamin, *beer retailer,* High
    street

Copeland, John, *innkeer,* Dog &
    Partridge, High street

Copeland, Thomas, *engraver,* Gate st

Copeland, Wm., *beer retailer*, Brunswick street

Cornes, James, *beer retailer*, Sun street

Cosgrove & Martin,
 britannia metal mounters of china & stone jugs, glass etc., Hanover street

Cotton, Emily (Mrs.), *dressmaker*, Hope street

Cottrell, Joseph, *beer retailer*, Great York street

Coulter, Margaret Ann (Mrs.),
 shopkeeper, Great York street

Coxon, Elijah, *greengrocer*, Marsh street

Coxon, John, *shopkeeper*, Windsor st

Coxon, John, *carpenter*, Cannon street

Craddock, William, *news agent*, Northwood

Crapper & Brierley, *dentists*, Broad st

Croston, William, *saddler*, Market street

Cruikshank, Ebenezer,
 boot & shoe warehouse, Piccadilly

Cunningham, Thomas,
 manager of National Provincial Bank of England, Market square

Curzon, Samuel, *shopkeeper*, Bucknall road

Cutts, James, *artist*, Snow hill

Dale, Charles, *boot & shoe maker*, Tontine street

Dale, George, *innkeer*, Black Swan, Stafford street

Dale, Josiah, *hay & straw dealer*, New st.

Dancer, Joseph, *baker*, Broad street

Daniel, John Coates, *accountant*, Stafford street

Daniel, J.C., see North Staffs Guardian Society

Daniel see Allbut & Daniel,

Daniel *see Sheardown & Daniel*

Dark, Richard Morgan, *hairdresser*, Well street

Davenport, Sampson, *boot & shoe maker*, Hope street

Davenport, Uriah, *linendraper*, Tontine square

Davenport see also Devonport

Davies, Evan,
 private teacher & accountant, Market street

Davies, John, *dyer*, Miles bank

Davis, Elijah, *crate maker*, Hope street

Davis, Francis,
 land & estate agent, & agent for the Hon. Edward Swynfen Parker Jervis, The Cottage, Well street

Davis, Joseph Barnard, M.D., *surgeon*, Albion street

Davis, Thomas, *innkeer*, White Hart, Etruria road

Davis, William, *gasfitter*, Tontine street

Davis, William Haslam, *surgeon*, Lamb st

Dawson, William, *beer retailer*, Lichfield street

Day, Joseph, *baker*, Hope street

Day, Joseph, *boot & shoe maker*, Market square

Dean, Ann (Mrs.), *milliner*, Piccadilly

Dean, Elizabeth (Mrs.), *linendraper*, Old Hall street

Dean, Frederick, *shopkeeper*, Well street

Devonport, James, *shopkeeper*, Tinker's clough

Dickens, Perrey, *innkeer*, Wheatsheaf Sheaf street

Dickin, Charles, *tinplate worker*, Market street

Dimmock, John & Co.,
 earthenware manufacturers of every description, Stafford street

Dix, Alexander Mills,
 common brewer & spirit merchant, Shelton brewery, Sun street

Dixon, John, *whip dealer*, Bucknall road

Dobbs, Thomas, *beer retailer*, Old Hall terrace

Docksey, John, *grocer*, Market square

Dodd, Thomas, *colour manufacturer*, Northwood

Doncaster, William, *baker*, Sun street

Doody, James, *beer retailer*,
Market street

Downs, James, *corn merchant*,
Chatterley house;
& at Stoke-upon-Trent

Draycott, Thomas, *innkeer*, Plough,
Etruria road

Draycott, Charles see Buller & Mugford

Dudson, James,
manufacturer of earthenware,
ornamental china figures,
improved Ironstone, china &
britannia metal mounted jugs
& colour for china, earthenware
& glass,
Hope street

Dunn, Thomas, *shopkeeper*,
Eastwood vale

Durose, Martha (Mrs.), *beer retailer*,
Eastwood vale

Dutton, Abraham, *watch & clock maker*,
High street

Dutton, Frederick, *butcher*, Northwood

Dutton, Henry, *baker*, Northwood

Dutton, Sarah (Miss), *dressmaker*,
Broad street

Eardley, Thomas, *saddler*,
Tontine street

Eastwood Mill Company,
flint merchants, grinders of
potters' materials, & ale &
porter merchants,[*]

Edge & Barlow, *corn & flour dealers*,
Broad st.reet & Piccadilly

Edge, John, *grocer*, Broom street

Edge, Thomas, *beer retailer*,
Bryan street

Edwards, Edward, *brush maker*,
Miles bank

Edwards, Richard, *innkeeper*,
Masons' Arms, North street

Edwards, Sarah (Miss), *milliner*,
Piccadilly

Edwards, William, *innkeeper*,
Fox & George, Hanover street

Eggington, Horatio, *joiner*,
Bucknall road

Eley, Charles, *beer retailer*, Etruria road

Elliott, Liddle, *engineer & manager*,
Staffordshire Potteries
Waterworks Co.,
Albion street

Ellis, George, *carpenter*, High street

Ellis, Hannah (Mrs.), *shopkeeper*,
Brunswick street

Ellis, Henry, *grocer*, Broad street

Ellis, James, *chemist & druggist*,
Broad street

Ellis, Richard, *grocer*, Greville street

Emery, Susan & Fanny (Misses),
milliners, Broad street

Emery, John, *portrait painter &*
photographic artist, Albion st

Emery, John, jun.,
pianoforte & music seller,
High street

Emery, Lewis, *shopkeeper*, Sun street

Espley, George, *turncock to North*
Staffordshire waterworks,
Chell street

Evans, Henry, *confectioner*, High street

Evens, John, *parian manufacturer, & gilder*
& decorator of earthenware &
china,   Hope street

Evans, William Lawrence, *chemist*,
Piccadilly

Evans *see Gibson & Evans*

Fairmann, John Bertram, *surgeon*,
Albion street

Falkner, William, *fruit dealer*,
Crown bank

Farmer, Charles, *boot & shoe maker*,
Marsh street

Farr, Thomas, *innkeeper*,
wine & spirit merchant
& inland revenue office,
Albion inn, Old Hall street

Farrell, Eliza (Mrs.), *tobacconist*, Broad st

Farrington, Thomas, *boot & shoe maker*,
Trinity street

Fearn, George, *clothier*, Market square

Fenton, Samuel, *potters' tool maker*,
Tontine passage

Fitton, Elizabeth (Mrs.), *clogger*,
Miles bank
Finney, Francis, *hairdresser*, Broad st
Finney, John, *butcher*, Broad street
Finney, Joseph F., *hairdresser*, Hope st.
Fletcher, Ellen (Mrs.), *nail maker*,
Piccadilly
Folker, William Henry, *surgeon*,
Market street
Forbes, Joseph Samuel, *surveyor to the
borough of Hanley*,
Shakespeare buildings
Forbes *see Stevens & Forbes*
Ford, Charles, *pin manufacturer*,
Herbert street
Ford, Thomas, *china manufacturer*,
Cannon street
Ford, William, *butcher*, Hope street
Ford see Potter & Ford
Forrester, David, *innkeeper*, King's Arms,
Broad street
Forrester, Joseph, *marine store dealer*,
Market street
Forrester, Richard Hammersley, *chemist*,
Market square
Forrester, William, *plumber*, High street
Fosbrook, Peter James, *tinplate worker*,
Piccadilly
Foster, Ann (Mrs.), *milliner*, New Hall st.
Foster, Henry, *commission agent*,
Albion place
Foulkes, Anne (Mrs.), *Shopkeeper*,
High street
Foulkes, Mary (Mrs.), *hosier*, Etruria road
Foulkes - see *Ridgway & Foulkes*
Fox, Joseph, *shopkeeper*, Hope street
Fradley, Solomon, *innkeeper*,
Bell & Bear, Snow hill
France, Mary Ann (Mrs.), *Milliner*,
Marsh street
Freeman, William, *grocer*, Northwood

Garner, Robert, *surgeon*, Winton villa
Gater, Thomas, *shopkeeper* *
Gee, John, *hosier*, George street
Gee, John, *marine store dealer*,
Swan passage

Gerrard, John (late) *see Goodwin,
Joseph*
Gibson & Evans, *ironmongers*,
Market square
Gibson, Elizabeth (Mrs.), *shopkeeper*,
Etruria road
Giles, Joseph, *shopkeeper*, Great York st
Gill, Rosa (Miss), *dressmaker*, Trinity st
Gilman, Thomas & Robert, *tailors*,
High street
Gilman, Thomas, *grocer*,
Piccadilly & Market square
Girdlestone, Horatio, *surgeon*, Albion st.
Gleeson, William, *joiner*, Pall mall
Glover, Arthur, *gunpowder agent*,
Albert place
Glover, James, *linendraper*, Broad street
Godwin, John, *cart owner*, Pall Mall
Godwin, John, *leather merchant*, Lamb st
Goldstraw, Matthew, *boot & shoe maker*,
Weaver street
Goldstraw, Ralph, *blacksmith*, Market st.
Goldstraw, Samuel, *plumber*, Stafford st.
Goldstraw, Thomas, *beer retailer*,
Union street
Goodhall, James, *beer retailer*, Market st.
Goodwin, Ellen (Miss), *school teacher*,
Lichfield street
Goodwin, George, *clothier*,
Broad street, Piccadilly
Goodwin, Joseph, *beer retailer*,
Broad street, Piccadilly
Goodwin, Joseph, *boot & shoe maker*,
Northwood
Goodwin, Joseph, *crate maker*,
Eastwood vale
Goodwin, Joseph W. (late John Gerrard),
*manufacturer of potters'
colours, glazes etc.*
Bath Street colour works
Goodwin, William,
paperhanging warehouse,
George street
Gould, Phoebe (Miss), *milliner*, Hope st.
Granville, Right Hon. Earl of,
iron & coal master,
Shelton colliery
Gray, Robert Henry, *tobacco pipe
maker*, Cannon street

Greaves, John, *shopkeeper*, High street
Greaves, William, *house & estate agent*,
    Broad street
Green, Herbert, *shopkeeper*, Broad st
Green *see Worthington & Green*
Greencamun, Thoms,
    Birmingham & Sheffield
    warehouse, Tontine street
Gresty, Thomas, beer retailer, Sun street
Griffiths, Jas., & Co.
    proprietors of turkish baths,
    Bagnall street
Griffiths, George B., *Hatter*,
    Parliament row
Griffiths, John, *shopkeeper*, Plough st
Grocott, John, *boot & shoe maker*,
    Northwood
Grosvenor, Edward, *grocer*, Broad street
Grosvenor, William, *surgeon*,
    Old Hall street
Guildford, Reuben, *hosier*, Piccadilly
Guilford, Edward, *boot & shoe maker*,
    Providence square

Hackney, Cordelia (Mrs.), *grocer*,
    Hope street
Hall, James, *beer retailer*, Hope street
Hall, Jane (Miss), *fancy repository*,
    Parliament row
Hall, John, *baker*, Broad street
Hall, John, *shopkeeper*, Bryan street
Hall, Joseph, *beer retailer*, Hope street
Hall, Richard, *beer retailer*,
    Tinker's clough
Hall, Roger, *innkeeper*, Old Crown inn,
    Crown bank
Hall, Thomas, *cabinet maker*, Marsh st
Hall, Thomas Hopkin, *beer retailer*,
    Marsh street
Hall, William, *wholesale & retail*
    wine & spirit dealer
    Piccadilly & Stafford street
Hambleton, William, *innkeeper*, Red
    Lion, Broad street
Hammersley, John, *pawnbroker*,
    High street
Hammersley, Robert, *carpenter*,
    Park street

Hammersley, Sarah (Mrs.), *shopkeeper*,
    High street
Hammond, Alphonso, *clothier*, Piccadilly
Hampton, Enoch, *innkeeper &*
    brickmaker,
    Duke of Wellington,
    Eastwood vale
Hancock, John, *innkeeper*,
    Royal Oak, Miles bank
Hand, Charles, *wheelwright*, Bucknall rd
Hand, William, *beer retailer*, Etruria road
Hanley Protestant Conservative
    Association & News Room,
    (Theophilus Pedley, hon. Sec.
    William Simpson, financial sec),
    Piccadilly
Hansell, Joseph, *beer retailer*, Sun street
Harding, William & Joseph,
    earthenware, egyptian black,
    rockingham stoneware, &
    ornamental & printed ware
    manufacturers,
    New Hall pottery
Harding, Richard, *turncock* to
    Staffordshire waterworks,
    Albion street
Harlow, Rebecca (Mrs.), *innkeeper*,
    Marquis of Granby,
    Crown bank
Harrington, William, *shopkeeper*,
    Brunswick street
Harris & Co, *clothiers*,
    Shakespeare buildings
Harris, Mary (Mrs.), *hosier*, High street
Harris, William Dean, *ironfounder*,
    Windmill street
Harrison, Charles, *grocer*, Marsh street
Harrison, Charlotte (Mrs.), *beer retailer*,
    Crown bank
Harrison, William, *tailor*, Market street
Harrop *see Worthington & Harrop*
Haslehurst, George, *hairdresser*,
    Tontine street
Haswell, John *see British Gas Light Co.*
Hassell, William, *secretary* to Potteries
    & Newcastle loan society,
    Cheapside
Hastings, Mary Ann (Mrs.),
    china & glass dealer, Piccadilly

Hawkins, Robert, *boot & shoe maker*,
Market street
Hawley, John, *shopkeeper*, Russell
street
Hawley, Richard, *coal dealer*, Sun street
Hawley, William, *greengrocer*,
Broad street
Haywood, James, *greengrocer*,
Hope street
Heap, James, *bookbinder*, Pall mall
Heap, William, *bookbinder*, Pall mall
Heath, Abraham & Charles, *plumbers*,
Cheapside
Heath, Ann Mare (Miss), *school teacher*,
Bucknall road
Heath, John, *crate maker*, Foundry field
Heath, Robert, *coal owner*
(Samuel Salt, agent), Russell st
Henshall, George, *artist*, Piccadilly
Henstock, Thomas, *currier, leather*
seller, closed uppers, lasts &
general grindery warehouse,
Parliament row
Hepworth & Co. *trade protection*
society, Shakespeare buildings
Hewitt, William, *grocer*, Piccadilly
Heylam, Josiah, *beer retailer*,
Russell street
Hibbert, William, *hatter*, Piccadilly
Hickin, Henry, *shopkeeper*,
Windmill street
Hickin, William, *gunsmith*, High street
Hill & Cooke, *pawnbrokers*, High street
Hill, Henry, *beer retailer*, Etruria vale
Hill, Thomas, *blacksmith*, Broad street
Hilton, Edward John, *crate maker*,
High street
Hilton, Joseph, *clogmaker*, Market street
Hodgkins, Samuel, *farrier*,
Great York street
Hodgkinson, Henry, *beer retailer*,
Eastwood vale
Hodkinson, Martha (Mrs.), *shopkeeper*,
Joiner's square
Holland, James, *coal dealer*,
Cauldon Place wharf
Hollins, John, *agent for Wm. Burn & Co.*
clay merchants, St. Austell,
Northwood

Hollins, John, *grocer & provision dealer*,
& post office receiving house,
Northwood
Hollins, John, *see Burn, William & Co.*
Hollowwood, John, *coal dealer*[x]
Holmes & Clarke, *brickmakers*, Sun st
Homer, Charles James Horatio,
land surveyor, Broom street
Hood, George, *earthenware*
manufacturer, Wharf lane
Hood, Thomas, *fruiterer*, Piccadilly
Hope, James, *Beer retailer*, Broad street
Hopkinson, Frederick, *shopkeeper*,
Eastwood vale
Hopwood, Joseph,
crate maker & beer retailer,
Winson street
Hopwood, William, *crate maker*,
Mollart street
Hordley, Thomas, *engraver*, Charles
street
Hordley, Thomas, *joiner*, Windsor street
Horne, Thomas, *wheelwright*, Etruria rd
Horne *see Stanway & Horne*
Horp, John, *beer retailer*, Eastwood vale
Howard, Joseph, *coffee rooms*,
Crown bank
Howlett, Emma (Mrs.), *dressmaker*,
Gill street
Howlett, John, *shopkeeper*, Gate street
Howlett, Sarah (Miss),
straw bonnet maker, Pall mall
Hughes, John Alfred, *decorative painter*,
Lamb street
Hughes, Mary (Mrs.), *confectioner*,
Tontine square
Hulme, George, *boot & shoe maker*,
Broom street
Hulse, Robert, *dining rooms*, High street
Humphreys, Edward, *baker*,
Great York street
Hunt, George, *stonemason*,
Chatterley bridge
Huntbach, Michael, *linendraper*,
Lamb street
Huston, William, *innkeeper*,
Dolphin, Piccadilly
Huston, Wilson, *egg merchant*,
Broad street

Iddins, John, B.A., *academy*, Greville street

Irwin, Thomas, *teadealer*, Northwood

Jackson, Edward, *ironfounder*, Old Hall street

James, John, *printer*, New street

James, William, *grocer*, Market square

Jaques, Samuel, *innkeeper*, Star, Marsh street

Jesper, Samuel, *clothier*, Market square

Johnson, Ambrose, *brushmaker*, Bryan street

Johnson, Catherine (Miss), *seminary*, Yale place

Johnson, Elijah, *newsagent*, Piccadilly

Johnson, James, *tinplate worker*, New Hall street

Johnson, Job, *boot & shoe maker*, Swan passage

Johnson, John, *boot & shoe maker*, Etruria road

Johnson, John, *bootmaker*, Hope street

Johnson, John, *boot & shoe maker*, Piccadilly

Johnson, John, *gasfitter*, Etruria road

Johnson, Richard, *shopkeeper & beer retailer*, Broad street

Johnson, William, *dining rooms*, Swan passage

Johnson, William, *stonemason*, Bryan street

Jones, Louisa & Rose (Misses), *milliners*, Broad street

Jones, Charles, *chemist*, Market square

Jones, Elijah, *auctioneer*, Lichfield street

Jones, John (Mrs.), *builder*, Albert place

Jones, Richard, *pork butcher*, Etruria rd

Jones, Robert, *shopkeeper*, Northwood

Jones, William, *butcher*, Tontine square

Joynson, William, *hosier*, Piccadilly

Keates, Charles, *pork butcher & sausage maker*, Market street

Keates, John, *collector of assessed taxes*, Cheapside

Keen *see Smith & Keen*

Keeling & Adams, *flint grinders*, Eastwood mill & Botteslow

Keeling, Ann (Miss), *dressmaker*, Union street

Keeling, James, *shopkeeper*, Union st

Keeling, William, *boot & shoe maker*, William street

Keen, Mark, *shopkeeper*, Marsh street

Kelsall, John, *beer retailer*, Bucknall rd

Kelsall, Joseph, *fishmonger*, Piccadilly

Kelsall, Mary (Mrs.), *beer retailer*, Abbey street

Kent, Charles, *beer retailer*, Great York street

Kent, George, *provision merchant*, Tontine street

Kenway, Luscombe & Co., *merchants & tallow chandlers*, Foundry Place wharf

Kenway, Luscombe & Co., *wholesale & retail tea dealers & grocers*, Fountain square

Kenyon, Thomas, *saw maker*, Stafford street

Kettle, William, *candle maker*, Charles street

Key, Josiah, *shopkeeper*, Marsh street

Keys, Joseph, *clogger*, Joiner's square

Kimberley, Thomas, *confectioner*, Tontine street

Kirk, George, *boiler maker*

Lacy, Rose (Mrs.), *tinplate worker*, Broad street

Lakin, Thomas, *shopkeeper*, Lower Charles street

Lamonby, Ann (Miss), *confectioner*, High street

Langley, Richard J., *ironmonger*, Piccadilly

Latham, William, *boot & shoe maker*, Old Hall street

Lawton, Alice (Miss), *dressmaker*, Lower Union street

Lawton, George, *beer retailer,*
Harley street
Lawton, Joseph, *boot & shoe maker,*
New street
Lawton, Martha (Mrs.), *shopkeeper,*
Lower Union street
Lawton, Thomas,
artificial fruit manufacturers,
Hope street.
Lawton, Thomas, *haberdasher,*
Broad street
Lawton, William, *china glass dealer,*
Broad street
Lawton, William Wright, *grocer,*
Market square
Lazarus, Benjamin & Co., *clothiers,*
Market square
Leader, Matthew, *shopkeeper,*
Northwood
Leak, Eliza (Mrs.) widow of the late
Emanuel Leak (William Henry
Walklet, manager),
*manufacturer of potters' lathes
& potters' tools of every
description,*
Church Street works
Leak, Leveson, *potters' lathe maker,*
King street
Leek, Charles, *boot & shoe maker,*
Hanover street
Leek, John, *boot & shoe maker,*
Bucknall road
Leek, Thomas, *clogger,* Marsh street
Lees, Ralph, *grocer,* Marsh street
Leib, Paul Solomon, *druggist,* Hope
street
Leigh, Enoch, *glass dealer,*
Tontine passage
Leonard, John, *builder,* Gate street
Lewis, John Benjamin, *dyer,* Stafford
street
Lightfoot, Elijah, *shopkeeper,*
Lower Hanover street
Litchfield, Henry, *furniture broker,*
Miles bank
Livesley, Powell & Co.,
*manufacturers of porcelain,
earthenware, pavan statuary &
china figures* (prize medal,
1862), Old Hall street & Miles
bank

Lloyd, Harriet (Mrs.), *dining rooms,*
Broad street
Lloyd, Isaac, *beer retailer,* High street
Lloyd, John, *chemist, druggist &
teadealer,* Piccadilly
Lomas, George, *shopkeeper,* Etruria rd
Lomas, William, *shopkeeper,*
Russell street
Loney, Samuel, *agent,* Howard place
Long, Henry, *butcher,* Piccadilly
Lovett, Michael, *cowkeeper,* Bucknall rd
Lucas, Alfred, *tailor,* Market street
Lunt, Samuel,
*innkeeper, & plumber &
painter,* Borough Arms, ,
Broad street
Luscombe Henry, *see Kenway,
Luscombe & Co*
Lyland, Patrick, *bath proprietor,*
Bryan street
Lyons, Isaac, *grocer,* Broad street
Lyons, Martin, *tinplate worker,*
Hope street

M

McBean, Alexander, *surgeon,*
New street
McCreery, James, *bookbinder,*
Church street
McDonald, George, *general dealer,*
Broad street
McDonald, Isabella (Mrs.), *milliner,*
High street
McGrail, Patrick, *greengrocer,* Miles
bank.
McLachlan, Robert, *beer retailer,*
Marsh street
Machin *see Steele & Machin*
Madden, Thomas, *beer retailer,*
Bryan street
Maddock, Thomas,
mining engineer & surveyor,
Bucknall Old road
Malkin, Elijah, *day school,* Eastwood
vale
Manchester Liverpool Banking Co.,
(James G. Walker, esq.
manager) (draw on Smith,
Payne & Smiths', London),
Market square

Mangnall, James, *beer retailer,*
Union street

Marsden & Son, *linendrapers,*
Market square

Marshall, Robert, *licensed to let horses,*
King street

Martin see Cosgrove & Martin

Massey, Emily (Mrs.), *butcher,*
Parliament row

Massey, Josiah, *fruiterer,* Brunswick st

Massey, Mary (Mrs.), *shopkeeper,*
Tinker's clough

Massey, Peter, *bootmaker,* Hope street

Massey, William Henry, *shopkeeper,*
Chell street

Matthews, Edward, *builder & contractor,*
New street

Matthews, George, jun., *butcher,*
Marsh street

Mayer, Joseph, *grocer,* Lamb street

Meakin, J. & G.,
earthenware manufacturers,
Eagle pottery

Meek, Benjamin Brown, *flour dealer,*
Parliament row

Meigh, George, *shopkeeper,* Sun street

Meigh, John Aynsley, *innkeeper,*
Lamb, Lamb street

Meigh, William Mellor,
smalt manufacturer,
Dresden works

Mellor, Samuel, jun. & Co., *dealers in*
glazed stoneware sewerage
pipes, waterclosets, firebricks,
terra cotta chimney pots,
vases, & roman & portland
cement; depot, Broad
street

Mellor, John, *boot & shoe maker,*
Hope street

Mellor, Margaret (Miss), *dressmaker,*
Tinker's clough

Mellor, Samuel, *butcher,*
Lower Hanover street

Mellor, Samuel junior, - see *Protector*
Endowment, Loan & Annuity
Company.

Mellor, Thomas, *academy,* New street

Mellor, Thomas, *wheelwright,* Etruria rd

Mellor, William, *builder,* Etruria road

Meredith, John, *tailor,* Bucknell road

Midlam, Sampson, *boot & shoe maker,*
Broad street

Miller, James, *furniture broker,*
Crown bank

Miller, John, *boot & shoe maker,*
Hanover street

Miller, John, *grocer,* Hope street

Millington, Francis, *boot & shoe maker,*
Mollart street

Mills, Elizabeth (Mrs.), *china*
manufacturer, George street

Mills, George, *brick & marl*
manufacturer, Cannon street

Mills, William Perry, *brewers' agent,*
King street

Millward, Henry, *baker,* Bryan Street

Mitchell, Stephen, *newsvendor,*
Miles bank

Moll, Henry, *basket maker,*
Piccadilly & Market square

Moore, Edward Thomas, *grocer,*
Tontine square

Moore, George Lennox, *surgeon,*
Shelton house

Moore see *Brown Westhead, Moore &*
Company

Moreton, Ralph, *hairdresser,* Bryan st

Morris, John, *innkeeper,* Antelope,
Trinity street

Mort, J. D. & C. C., *printers & publishers*
Staffordshire Advertiser,
Piccadilly

Moseley, William Henry, *dairy,*
Tontine street

Mountford, Jno., *general merchant,*
New Park villa & Trentham

Mountford, Mary (Mrs.),
straw bonnet maker,
Northwood

Mountford, Prudence (Mrs.), *teadealer,*
Norfolk street

Mountford, Samuel, *shopkeeper,*
High street

Monntford see *Unwin, Monntford &*
Taylor

Moxon, James, *solicitor,* Brunswick
street

Mugford *see Buller & Mugford*
Mulliner, Henry, *beer retailer*,
    Brunswick street
Murrells, Joseph *see Bailey, Murrells & Co*
Mycock & Son, flint mill, Hope street

Narramore, Robert Edwin,
    commission agent, King street
National Provincial Bank of England
    (Thomas Cunningham,
    manager) (draw on Hanbury &
    Co.),   Market sq
New Mechanics' Institute, Pall mall
Nicholls, T. & R., *timber merchants*,
    Mill street, Etruria road, and at
    Wharf street, Stoke-upon-Trent
Nicholls, Henry, *chemist*, Market square
Nicholls, Henry, *shopkeeper*, Hill street
Nicklin, Henry, *cabinet maker*, Piccadilly
Nicklin, Lewis, *cabinet maker*,
    Parliament row
Nicklin, Sarah Ann (Mrs.), *milliner*,
    Bethesda street
Nicklin, William, *beer retailer*,
    St. Luke street
Nixon, Henry, *tailor*, Hope street.
Norbury, John, *beer retailer*, Union st
North Staffordshire Guardian Society for
    the Protection of Trade
    (John C. Daniel, sec.)
Norton, William, *blacking manufacturer*,
    Piccadilly
Nunns, James, *wire worker*, Broad street
Nutt, George, *boot & shoe warehouse*,
    High street

Ogden, James, *builder*, Harley street
Old Hall Earthenware Co. (limited),
    *manufacturers of every
    description of earthenware &
    china*,
    Old Hall street
Oldham, James,
    earthenware manufacturer,
    Bethesda street
Osmond, Charles Marsh, *academy*,
    Richmond terrace

Owens, Edward, *shopkeeper*,
    Broom street.

Paddock, George, jun., *solicitor*,
    Miles bank
Painter, Frederick, *commercial traveller*,
    Broom street
Palin, Ann (Mrs.), *greengrocer*, New st
Palin, James, *innkeeper*, Trumpet inn,
    Parliament row
Palmer, Henry, *saw mills*, Gate street
Palmer, Richard, *clothes dealer*,
    Broad street
Palmer, Thomas, *innkeeper*,
    Bell, Broad street
Palmer, William Turner, *architect*,
    Church street
Pankhurst & Co.,
    earthenware manufacturers,
    Old Hall street
Parkes, Ebenezer, *chemist*, Piccadilly
Parkinson & Son, *chimney sweepers*,
    New street
Parkinson, Ann (Mrs.),
    blacking manufacturer,
    Lamb street
Parr & Taylor (Misses),
    straw bonnet makers,
    Piccadilly
Parrish, Thomas, *beer retailer*,
    Bryan street
Parton, Henry, *shopkeeper*, Hope street
Pass, John, *cooper*, Stafford street
Paton, John, *shopkeeper*, Northwood
Pauley, William, *furniture broker*, Great
    York street
Peake, John Machil, *commercial
    traveller*, Tinker's clough
Peake, Joseph, *hay & straw dealer*,
    Broad street
Peake, Samuel, *shopkeeper*,
    St. Luke street
Pearce, James, *beer retailer*, Stafford
    street
Pedley, James, *shopkeeper*, Harley
    street

Pedley, Theophilus *see Hanley Protestant Conservative Association*

Pembleton, Sarah (Mrs.), *shopkeeper*, Etruria road

Penney, Harriet (Mrs.), *innkeeper*, White Lion, High street

Pennington, Charles, *china dealer*, Old Hall street

Penton *see Woolliscroft & Penton*

Pepper, Elisha, *engraver*, Well street

Perry, Hannah (Mrs.), *shopkeeper*, Bucknall road

Perry, John, *shopkeeper*, Sheaf street

Perry, Joseph, *cutler*, Broad street

Picken, James, *hairdresser*, Piccadilly

Pickering, Henry, *shopkeeper*, St. Mark's street

Pidduck, Henry, *watchmaker & jeweller*, Market square

Pidduck, Thomas, *ironmonger*, Tontine square

Pierce, Edward, *boot & shoe maker*, Northwood

Pierce, Edward Lloyd, *druggist*, Piccadilly

Pierpoint, James, *beer retailer*, Well street

Plant, Henry, *shopkeeper*, Eastwood vale

Platt, Henry, *innkeeper*, Eagle & Child, Etruria road

Platt, John Spalton, *grocer & teadealer*, Broad street

Pointon, Aaron, *shopkeeper*, Russell street

Pointon, Martha (Mrs.), *milliner*, Hope street

Poitevin, Edward, *soda water, lemonade, apple wine, cider & medicated water manufacturer, & importer of aromatic dutch bitters, cordials etc.* Bryan street

Pool, Isaac, *boot & shoe maker*, Swan street

Poole, Hamlet, *shopkeeper*, St. Mark's street

Poole, Hamlet, jun. *boot & shoe maker*, Northwood

Poole, Richard, *draper*, Broom street

Poole, Sarah (Mrs.), *shopkeeper*, Broom street

Pope, Frederick, *carpenter*, High street

Pope, William, *engraver*, Pall mall

Potter & Ford, *printers*, Cheapside

Potter, Thomas Andrew, *proprietor and publisher : The 'Sentinel'* Cheapside

Potteries & Newcastle loan society (William Hassell secretary), Cheapside

Pottery Mechanics' Institution & North Staffordshire Museum (E. Brunt, secretary & librarian), Pall mall

Potts, Thomas, *cabinet maker*, Piccadilly

Potts, William, *cabinet maker*, Broad st

Poulson, John, *colour maker*, Lichfield street

Presbury, William, *shopkeeper*, Market street

Prince, William, *cowkeeper*, Bucknall road

Protector Endowment, Loan & Annuity Company (Samuel Mellor, jun. manager) Broad street

Quoroll, John, *smallware dealer*, High street

Radford, John, *tailor*, John street

Ratcliff, George, *shopkeeper*, Old Hall street

Ratcliff, William, *beer retailer*, Joiner's square

Ratcliffe, Henry, *baker*, Windsor street

Redfern, John, *builder*, Bryan street

Redfern, John Ellis, *shopkeeper*, Edmund street

Redfern, Mary (Mrs.), *stationer*, Broad street

Richardson, Isaac, *grocer*, High street

Richardson, Samuel, *baker*, Vine street

Ridgway & Foulkes, *grocers*, Tontine street

Ridgway, Edward John,
    earthenware manufacturer,
    High street
Ridgway, George, *grocer*, Swan passage
Ridgway, Thomas, *shopkeeper*,
    Cobden street
Rigby, John, *newsvendor*, Etruria road
Rigby, Samuel, *innkeeper*,
    French Horn, Crown bank
Riles, Eliza (Miss), *milliner*, High street
Riley, Charles, *beer retailer*,
    Old Hall street
Riley, Thomas, *butcher*, Broad street
Ringland, Hans, *linendraper*,
    Stafford street
Rivers, William Mollart,
    watchmaker & jeweller,
    Hope st
Roberts, Daniel, *shopkeeper*,
    Great York street
Roberts, John, *shopkeeper*,
    Tinker's clough
Roberts, Josiah, *boot & shoe maker*,
    Stafford street
Roberts, Thomas, *beer retailer*,
    Tontine Street
Robey, Clement, *accountant*,
    Old Hall street
Robinson, James & Co., *drapers*,
    Market square
Robinson, James, *shopkeeper*, Hill street
Robinson, Jane (Miss),
    milliner & dressmaker, Pall mall
Robinson, William, *confectioner*,
    Piccadilly
Robson, Henry, *umbrella maker*,
    Market street
Rochell, Hannah (Mrs.), *provision dealer*,
    Tontine street
Rock, Thomas, *fishmonger*, Piccadilly
Roden, Jane (Miss), *staymaker*,
    Hanover street
Roden, William S., *manager :*
    Shelton bar iron company,
    Etruria road
Roe, Henry & Son, *parian figure makers*,
    Bow street
Roper, Francis, *beer retailer*, Broom st
Rourke, Luke, *beer retailer*, Marsh street

Rowe, John, *shoemaker*, Greville street
Rowland, George, *fruiterer*, Old Hall st
Rowley & Co., *skin dealers*, Swan
    passage
Rowley, John Broadfield & Co.,
    homæopathic chemists &
    agents for James Epps'
    homæopathic cocoa & Charles
    Macintosh & Co.'s India rubber
    goods Terrace buildings,
    Market square
Rowley, Bagnall, *innkeeper*,
    New inn, New street
Rowley, John, *shopkeeper*, Northwood
Roycroft, Henry, *coach builder*,
    Albion street
Ruscoe, Joseph, *boot & shoe maker*,
    Tinker's clough
Rushton, John, *butcher*, Hope street
Rushton, John, *butcher*, Piccadilly
Rushton, Robert, *crate maker & cooper*,
    Charles street, & cooperage,
    Copeland street, Stoke
Rushton, William, *draper*, Hope street
Rushton, William, *milliner*, Piccadilly
Ryder, David, *coal dealer*, wood street

S

Sadler, Edward, *cabinet maker*,
    Piccadilly
Salmon, Eliza (Mrs.), *milliner*,
    Brunswick street
Salmon, James, *grocer*, Piccadilly
Salmons, Thomas, *hairdresser*, Piccadilly
Salt, Charles, *parian manufacturer*,
    Bethesda street
Salt, Francis, *confectioner*, Market street
Salt, John, *blacksmith*, Etruria road
Salt, John, *crate maker*, Hill street
Salt, Samuel, *agent for Robert Heath*,
    (coal owner), Russell st
Sands, Thomas, *hosier*, Tontine street
Sant, Thomas, *boot & shoe maker*,
    New Hall street
Sargeant, Charles, *shopkeeper*,
    Hope street
Sargeant, Thomas, *butcher*,
    New Hall street

Sawyer, James, *innkeeper,*
  George & Dragon, New street
Sawyer, John, *beer retailer,* High street
Scarlett, William, *chemist & druggist,*
  Market square
Scarratt & Bickley, *plumbers,* Piccadilly
Scarratt, George, *plumber & painter,*
  Piccadilly.
Scarratt, Joseph, *plumber,* Albion street
Schofield, Robert, *innkeeper,*
  Roebuck, Piccadilly
Scott, Henry, *surgeon,* Albion street
Scott, James, *boot & shoe maker,*
  High street
Scrivener, Robert, *architect & surveyor,*
  Howard place
Seaburn, Joseph, *boot & shoe maker,*
  Tinker's clough
Sedgley, Eliza (Miss), *milliner,* Well
  street
Sedgley, Mary (Miss), *school,* Well
  street
Sedgley, William, *plumber,* Well street
Sergeant, George, *commission* agent,
  Grove cottage
Shaw, George, *cutler,* Tontine street
Shaw, Richard, *grocer & provision*
  dealer, Broad street
Shaw, Thomas Cotterill, *surveyor,*
  Bucknall road
Shaw, William, *beer retailer,*
  Great York street
Sheardown & Daniel, *printers,* John
  street
Sheldon, James, *shopkeeper,*
  Edmund street
Shelley, Sampson Astbury,
  camelhair pencil maker,
  Pall mall
Shelton Bar Iron Co., (prize medal,
  1862), *ironmasters & ironworks*
  (William S. Roden, manager) ;
  works, Etruria road ; London
  office 38 Dowgate hill E C
Shelton Colliery & Iron Works,
  (Frederick Wragge, agent),
  Etruria road
Sherratt, Hugh Hulme, *grocer,* Piccadilly

Sherwin, Enoch, *beer retailer,*
  Stafford street
Sherwin, Henry, *shopkeeper,* Broad st
Sherwin, Robert,
  wholesale brush manufacturer,
  New street
Sherwin, William, *boot & shoe maker,*
  Gill street
Shipley, Edward, *butcher,* Lichfield st
Shipley, Thomas, *shopkeeper,* Etruria rd
Shirley, William, *shopkeeper,* Bryan st
Shotton, Samuel, *butcher,* Sheaf street
Shuttlebotham, John, *grocer,*
  Parliament row
Shuttlebotham, James, *coal dealer,*
  Hanover street
Sidley, William, *furniture broker,* High st
Silvester, William, *tailor,* Tontine street
Simms, William, *beer retailer,*
  Great York street
Simpson, Elizabeth (Mrs.), *shopkeeper,*
  New Hall street
Simpson, George, *hay & straw dealer,*
  New Hall street
Simpson, Henry, *butcher,* Piccadilly
Simpson, Kitty Maria (Miss), *milliner,*
  Eastwood vale
Simpson, Robert, *hairdresser,*
  Tontine street
Simpson, Thomas, *fruiterer,* Broad street
Simpson, William, *financial secretary :*
  Hanley Protestant Conservative
  Association, Piccadilly
Skarratt, Josiah, *boot & shoe maker,*
  Union street
Slaney, John, *commission agent,*
  Windsor street
Slater, John, *beer retailer,* Chapel street
Slater, Thomas, *innkeeper,*
  Black Horse, Great York street
Smith & Keen, *tobacco manufacturers,*
  Bryan street
Smith & Sons, *wood turners,* Trinity st
Smith, Charles John, *coal & iron master*
Smith, Edward, *shopkeeper,* Well street
Smith, Edwin John, *beer retailer,*
  Sun street
Smith, George, *butcher,* Union street

Smith, George, *painter*, Broad street
Smith, Herbert, *cabinet & general furniture manufacturer*, Piccadilly
Smith, John, *parian maker*, Hope street
Smith, John, *shopkeeper*, Broom street
Smith, John Henry, *innkeeper*, Three Tuns, Bucknall road
Smith, Samuel, *beer retailer*, Marsh st
Smith, Samuel, *beer retailer*, Well street
Smith, Theophilus, *tailor*, High street
Smith, Thomas, *butcher*, Broad street
Smith, William, *newsvendor*, Brunswick street
Smytheman, William, *shopkeeper*, Stafford street
Sneyd, James, *shopkeeper*, Well street
Snook, Jonah, *clothier*, Northwood
Snow, John, *greengrocer*, Broad street
Solomon see Benjamin Solomon & Co.
Spencer, Henry, *grocer*, Marsh street
Spencer, John, *ironmonger*, Marsh street
Spencer, John, *tailor*, Hanover street
Spilsbury, William, *photographer*, Stafford street
Staffordshire Advertiser, (branch office) (J. D. & C. C. Mort, printers & publishers), Piccadilly
Staffordshire Potteries Loan Society, (Henry Cartledge, sec.), Miles bank
Staffordshire Potteries Street Railway Co. (Edward Henry Brassington, sec, pro. Tern.), Trinity street
Staffordshire Potteries Waterworks Co., (Liddle Elliott, engineer & manager. Charles Baines, secretary), Albion street
Staffordshire Sentinel, (Thomas Andrew Potter, printer & publisher), Cheapside
Stanley, John, *beer retailer*, Hope street
Stanley, John, *shopkeeper*, Sheaf street
Stanton, John, *fruiterer*, Tontine street
Stanway & Horne, *parian makers & stonemasons*, Eastwood vale

Stanway, Amy (Mrs.), *milliner & straw bonnet maker*, Etruria road
Stanway, William, *cooper*, Miles bank
Statham, George Leveridge, *circulating library*, Lamb street
Steele & Machin, *pawnbrokers*, New Hall street
Steele, James, *clothier*, Piccadilly
Steele, John, *builder*, St. Luke's street
Steele, William, *shopkeeper*, Bryan street
Stephenson, Joseph, *manufacturer of colours for china, earthenware & glass*, Bethesda street
Stephenson, Naomi (Mrs.), *milliner & dressmaker*, Lamb st
Stevens & Forbes, *architects & surveyors* of Manchester, Macclesfield & Hanley, Shakespeare buildings
Stevenson, John, *clockmaker*, Hope street
Stevenson, Josiah, *draper*, Lichfield street
Stevenson, Ralph, *solicitor*, Bagnall street
Stokes, Thomas, *tailor*, Broad street
Stonier, Thomas, *collector of poor rates for Sheldon district*, Albion st.
Stonier, William, *beer retailer*, Bryan street
Stonier, William, *brickmaker*, Bucknall road
Storey, Henry William, *artists' brush maker*, Well street
Stranaghan, Elizabeth (Mrs), *provision dealer*, Piccadilly
Stranaghan, James, *provision merchant*, Stafford street
Streete, Henry John, *grocer*, Piccadilly
Stubbs, Christopher, *innkeeper*, Black Horse, Bucknall road
Stubbs, Enoch, *beer retailer*, Abbey street
Stubbs, Herbert, *coal dealer*, Abbey st.
Stubbs, Samuel, *beer retailer*, Well street

Stubbs, William, *manufacturer of china & earthenware, egyptian black, stoneware, parian, lustre, figures & ornaments,* Eastwood pottery

Sunnington, James, *crate maker,* Hope street

Sutherland, Daniel, *carver & gilder,* Tontine street

Sutton, Charles, *fruit & potato merchant,* Parliament row

Sutton, Elizabeth (Miss), *tobacconist,* Hope street

Sutton, Thomas, *beer retailer,* Market street

Sutton, William, *butcher,* Great York street

Swetman, Henry, *beer retailer,* Broad street

Swetman, John Hassall, *pawnbroker & clothier,* Trinity street

Swift, Ann (Mrs.), *beer retailer,* Etruria rd

Swift, Henry, *innkeeper,* Saracen's Head commercial hotel & posting house, & wine & spirit merchant fly, omnibus & funeral carriage proprietor; omnibus to Stoke to meet all trains, Stafford street & Piccadilly

Swift, Thomas, *linendraper,* Market square

T abbinor, Samuel, *beer retailer,* Bow street

Taylor, Brothers & Co., *earthenware manufacturers,* Market street

Taylor, Ann (Mrs.), *straw bonnet maker,* Hill street

Taylor, Elizabeth (Miss), *straw bonnet maker,* Parliament row

Taylor, George, *coal dealer,* Bow street

Taylor, James, *herbalist & botanist,* Broad street, & New Market terrace, Longton

Taylor, Thomas, *shopkeeper,* Marsh st

Taylor, William, *granite earthenware manufacturer, for home & exportation* ; works, Brook street

Taylor, William, *lead merchant,* Park villa

Taylor *see Unwin, Monntford & Taylor*

Taylor (Miss) see Parr & Taylor

Tennant, Edmund, *solicitor,* Cheapside

The Enamel Porcelain Co. (limited), Old Hall street

Thomas, Joseph, *clock maker,* Crown bank

Thompson, Henry, *shopkeeper,* Eastwood vale

Thorley, Elizabeth (Mrs.), *milliner,* King street

Thorley, William, *butcher,* Joiner's square

Thorpe, Thomas, *shopkeeper,* Hill street

Till & Brown, *shopkeepers,* Hill street

Till, Benjamin, *blacksmith,* Cannon street

Till, John, *shopkeeper,* Bryan street

Till, Mary (Mrs.), *blacksmith,* Broad street

Till, Rupert, *wood turner,* Brunswick st

Timmis, William, *bookseller,* Market square

Tittensor, George, *hosier,* High street

Toft, Thomas, *engraver,* Albion street

Toft, Thomas, *watchmaker,* Bucknall rd

Tomlinson, Thomas, *boot & shoe maker,* Parliament row

Tourton, Claudius, *professor of french,* Snow hill

Toussaint, Edward & Co., *wholesale & retail tobacconists,* Piccadilly

Tristram, Josiah, *confectioner,* Piccadilly

Tunnicliffe, Abraham, *beer retailer,* Foundry fields

Tunstall, John, *boot & shoe maker,* Free Trade street

Turner, Charles, *innkeeper,* King's Head commercial inn & posting house, & *wine & spirit merchant,* Piccadilly

Turner, Edward, *haberdasher*,
    Marsh street
Turner, John, *butcher*, North street
Twigg, George, *beer retailer*,
    Old Hall street
Twigg, George, *shopkeeper*, Etruria road
Twyford, Christopher, *innkeeper*, Talbot,
    Market street
Twyford, Thomas, *earthenware*
    manufacturer, Bath street

U nwin, Monntford & Taylor,
    earthenware manufacturers,
    Upper Hanley works

V enables, Henry, *jasper maker*,
    Etruria road
Vessey, Thomas Watson, *pawnbroker*,
    Broad street
Vigers, John, *coal dealer*, Wood street
Vigers, John,
    corn dealer, grocer & teadealer,
    Broad street
Vyse, Thomas, *bootmaker*, Lamb street

W akefield, Thomas, *cabinet maker*,
    Hanover street
Walker, James, *modeller*, High street
Walker, James G., *manager* of the
    Manchester & Liverpool
    banking company,
    Market square
Walker, John, *crate maker*,
    Eastwood vale
Walker, John Swift, *surgeon*,
    Old Hall terrace
Walker, Joseph, *beer retailer*, Northwood
Walker, William, *shopkeeper*, Bow street
Walklet, William H., *britannia metal*
    manufacturer, china &
    earthenware mounter,
    wholesale and for exportation,
    Church Street Works
Walklet, Henry William, *hosier*,
    Parliament row
Walklet, William Henry see Eliza Leak

Walker, James G., see Manchester
    Liverpool Banking Co.
Wallace, James, *tailor*, Hill street
Walley, John, *china & ornamental parian*
    manufacturer,
    Hope street
Walley, Mary (Mrs.), *grocer*, Hope street
Walley, Noah, *shopkeeper*, Etruria road
Walley, Titus, *shopkeeper*, St.
    Mark's street
Walley, William Thomas, *cheese factor*,
    Market square
Wallworth, James, *currier*, Old Hall street
Walthall, William, *hairdresser*,
    Market square,
Walton, William, *auctioneer*, Miles bank
Ward, Son & Co., *Architects*,
    Albion house
Ward, Henry, *brickmaker*. Bucknall road
Ward, Louisa (Miss), *milliner*, Hope st
Wardle & Ash,
    manufacturers of ornamental
    parian, stone & coloured
    bodies,
    Broad street
Wardle, George, *cooper*, Crown bank
Wardle, Joseph, *boot & shoe maker*,
    Charles street
Warner, John, *engineer*, George street
Warner, Robert, *beer retailer*,
    Cobden street
Warner, Thomas, *beer retailer*,
    Hope street
Warner, William, *baker*, Lichfield street
Warrillow, Anthony, *butcher*, High street
Warrington, William & Co.,
    parian makers,
    Brewery street
Warrington, John Thomas, *cheese*
    factor, Miles bank
Warrington, William, *shopkeeper*,
    Joiner's square
Wase, Esther (Mrs.), *egg dealer*,
    Marsh street
Weaver, Thomas, *beer retailer*,
    Northwood
Wedgwood, John, *hairdresser*,
    Market street

Welch, John, *watch & clock maker*,
Albion street

Wells, George, *grocer*, Bath street

Weston, Charles, *beer retailer*,
Bath street

Wevar, William, *beer retailer*, Gate street

Wheeler, Martin, *innkeeper*,
Crown & Anchor, New Hall st

Whiston, James, *beer retailer*, Bryan st

White, William, *greengrocer*,
Hope street

Whitehead, Joseph, *bootmaker*,
Brunswick street

Whitehead, Joseph, *boot & shoe maker*,
Tontine street

Whitehead, William, *clogger*,
Bryan street

Whittingham & Son,
*auctioneers, appraisers,
upholsterers, cabinet makers &
wholesale & retail
paperhanging warehouse*,
Albion street

Whittingham, John Fowler,
*professor of music (from the
College of Music, Stuttgart, &
sole agent for the county of
Staffordshire for Messrs.
Schiedmayer's (of Stuttgart),
pianofortes & harmoniums*,
Albion street

Wilbraham, Thomas, *news agent*,
Hope street

Wilkinson & Sons,
*porcelain, china & ornamental
parian manufacturers*,
Havelock works,
Broad street

Wilkinson, Edwin, *hairdresser*,
Marsh street

Wilkinson, John, *ale & porter merchant*,
stores 7 & 9 Hope st

Wilkinson, John, *innkeeper*,
George & Dragon, New street

Williams, David, *shopkeeper*, Hope
street

Williams, David, *tailor*, Hanover street

Williams, Henry, *confectioner*,
Miles bank

Williams, John, *beer retailer*,
Great York street

Willshaw, George, *beer retailer*,
Miles bank

Wilson, Edward, *shopkeeper*,
Regent street

Wilson, William, *chemist*, High street

Wilson, William Joseph, *bootmaker*,
Broad street

Winfield, John, *toy dealer*, Hope street

Winter, John, *beer retailer*, Russell street

Wood & Son, *general merchants*,
Broad street

Wood, George, *innkeeper*,
Roebuck, Hope street

Wood, Joel, *boot & shoe maker*,
Victor street

Woodward, Charles, *boot & shoe maker*,
King street

Woodward, John, *shopkeeper*,
Bryan street

Woodward, Thomas, *farmer*, Bank farm

Wooldridge, Clement, *builder*,
Broad street.

Wooldridge, Edward, *butcher*,
Broad street

Wooldridge, Richard, *innkeeper*,
Jug inn, Broad street

Woolley, Thomas, *tailor & hatter*,
Tontine square

Woolliscroft & Penton, *plumbers*,
Broad street

Woolliscroft, Harding, *baker*, Marsh st

Woolliscroft, William, *tobacconist*,
Piccadilly

Worthington & Green,
china figure manufacturers,
Booden brook

Worthington & Harrop,
*ornamental china figure
manufacturers*,
Tinker's clough

Worthington & Son,
*earthenware etc.
manufacturers*, Clarence st

Worthington, Samuel,
*innkeeper, brewer & spirit
merchant*,
Red Lion inn, New street

Wragge, Frederick, *agent to Shelton colliery & ironworks,* Etruria road

Wray, Joseph, *marine store dealer,* Miles bank

Wray, Mary (Mrs.), *beer retailer,* Union street

Wright, Benjamin, *innkeeper,* Plough, High street

Wright, John, *shopkeeper,* Eastwood vale

Wright, Joseph, *grocer,* Market square

Wright, Susan (Miss), *religious tract depot,* Albion street

Wright, William, *chemist,* Northwood

Wright, William, *shopkeeper,* Eastwood vale

Wyatt, Lewis, *clock & watch maker,* Piccadilly

Y ates, James, *beer retailer,* Swan street

Yates, Samuel, *shopkeeper,* Great York street

Yates, Sarah (Mrs.), *beer retailer,* Brunswick street

Yates, William, *colliery owner,* Ivy House colliery

Yates, William Henry, *chemist,* Lamb street

Yellard, Almond, *cooper,* Tontine passage

Hanley in 1864

From page 4

The Independents, Presbyterians, Baptists, Wesleyan, and New Connexion Methodists have chapels in the town; one belonging to the latter body; called Bethesda, situated in Albion-street, is a very large building.

There are a British and two. National schools, an evening school, and a ragged school, besides several day, infant and Sunday schools in connection with the churches and dissenting chapels.

The Government School of Design, in Pall Mall, was established in 1847. The Pottery Mechanics' Institution and North Staffordshire Museum, in Frederick-street, founded in 1825, has a valuable library, and a reading-room well supplied with periodicals. The Mechanics' Institution has a spacious and elegant new building in course of erection, (at an estimated cost of £3,000), on a more central and commanding site, adjacent to the British school.

Continued on page 43

Classified

Accountants
Daniel, John Coates
Robey, Clement

Administration, Law enforcement etc
Brown, Hugh
Challinor, Edward
Cole, Samuel
Farr, Thomas
Hollins, John
Keates, John
Stonier, Thomas

Agents
Butterworth, John
Collison, Thos.
Hollins, John
Loney, Samuel

Ale & porter merchants
Wilkinson, John
Eastwood Mill Company

Appraisers
Whittingham & Son

Architects
Palmer, William Turner
Scrivener, Robert
Stevens & Forbes
Ward Son & Co.

Artificial Fruit Manufacturers
Lawton, Thomas

Artists
Allen, Thomas
Cutts, James
Henshall, George

Auctioneers
Booth, George
Jones, Elijah
Walton, William
Whittingham & Son

Bakers
Beech, William
Bickerton, Thomas
Bishop, James
Clark, George
Dancer, Joseph
Day, Joseph
Doncaster, William
Dutton, Henry
Hall, John
Humphreys, Edward
Millward, Henry
Ratcliffe, Henry
Richardson, Samuel
Warner, William
Woolliscroft, Harding

Bankers etc
Cunningham, Thomas
Manchester Liverpool Banking Co.
National Provincial Bank of England
Protector Endowment, Loan & Annuity Co.

Basket Makers
Barcroft, John
Barcroft, Charles
Moll, Henry

Bath Proprietors
Griffiths, Jas. & Co.
Lyland, Patrick

Beer Machine Handle Maker
Buckley, John

Beer Retailers
Arkley, Mary (Mrs.)
Bailey, John
Ball, Thomas
Barlow, Rebecca (Mrs.)
Barrett, David
Bartholomew, Sarah (Mrs.)
Bate, James
Beech, George
Belfield, Ann (Mrs.)
Bladun, Edward
Blakeman, Henry
Bloor, Francis Elijah
Boon, Edward
Boulton, John
Carpmail, Moses
Challinor, Samuel
Charlesworth, William
Cherry, Joseph
Cliff, Robert
Colclough, Benjamin
Colclough, Elizabeth (Mrs.)
Cooper, Ellen (Miss)
Copeland, Wm.
Copeland, Benjamin
Cornes, James
Cottrell, Joseph
Dawson, William
Dobbs, Thomas
Doody, James
Durose, Martha (Mrs.)
Edge, Thomas
Eley, Charles
Goldstraw, Thomas
Goodhall, James
Goodwin, Joseph
Gresty, Thomas
Hall, Richard

Hall, James
Hall, Joseph
Hall, Thomas Hopkin
Hand, William
Hansell, Joseph
Harrison, Charlotte (Mrs.)
Heylam, Josiah
Hill, Henry
Hodgkinson, Henry
Hope, James
Hopwood, Joseph
Horp, John
Johnson, Richard
Kelsall, John
Kelsall, Mary (Mrs.)
Kent, Charles
Lawton, George
Lloyd, Isaac
Madden, Thomas
Mangnall, James
McLachlan, Robert
Mulliner, Henry
Nicklin, William
Norbury, John
Parrish, Thomas
Pearce, James
Pierpoint, James
Ratcliff, William
Riley, Charles
Roberts, Thomas
Roper, Francis
Rourke, Luke
Sawyer, John
Shaw, William
Sherwin, Enoch
Simms, William
Slater, John
Smith, Samuel
Smith, Samuel
Smith, Edwin John
Stanley, John
Stonier, William
Stubbs, Enoch
Stubbs, Samuel
Sutton, Thomas
Swetman, Henry
Swift, Ann (Mrs.)
Tabbinor, Samuel
Tunnicliffe, Abraham
Twigg, George

Walker, Joseph
Warner, Robert
Warner, Thomas
Weaver, Thomas
Weston, Charles
Wever, William
Whiston, James
Williams, John
Willshaw, George
Winter, John
Wray, Mary (Mrs.)
Yates, James
Yates, Sarah (Mrs.)

Blacking Manufacturers
Norton, William
Parkinson, Ann (Mrs.)
Stubbs, William
Blacksmiths
Berrisford, Henry
Burndred, James
Goldstraw, Ralph
Hill, Thomas
Salt, John
Till, Benjamin
Till, Mary (Mrs.)

Boiler Makers
Barrow, John
Kirk, George

Bookbinders
Heap, James
Heap, William
McCreery, James

Booksellers
Allbut & Daniel
Bebbington, James
Timmis, William
Boot & Shoe Makers
Bates, Cornelius
Beeteson, Edne (Mrs.)
Blakeley, William
Boston, John
Broom, Elizabeth (Mrs.)
Carr, George
Cartlidge, Joseph
Chetwin, Joseph
Clarke, William

Cope, Thomas
Dale, Charles
Davenport, Sampson
Day, Joseph
Farmer Charles
Farrington, Thomas
Goldstraw, Matthew
Goodwin, Joseph
Grocott, John
Guilford, Edward
Hawkins, Robert
Hulme, George
Johnson, Job
Johnson, John
Johnson, John
Johnson, John
Keeling, William
Latham, William
Lawton, Joseph
Leek, Charles
Leek, John
Massey, Peter
Mellor, John
Midlam, Sampson
Miller, John
Millington, Francis
Pierce, Edward
Pool, Isaac
Poole, Hamlet jun
Roberts, Josiah
Rowe, John
Ruscoe, Joseph
Sant, Thomas
Scott, James
Seaburn, Joseph
Sherwin, William
Skarratt, Josiah
Tomlinson, Thomas
Tunstall, John
Vyse, Thomas
Wardle, Joseph
Whitehead Joseph
Whitehead, Joseph
Wilson, William Joseph
Wood, Joel
Woodward, Charles

Boot & shoe warehouses
Cruikshank, Ebenezer
Nutt, George

Brewers & brewers' agents
Dix, Alexander Mills
Mills, William Perry
Worthington, Samuel

Bricklayers
Austin, Joseph
Bryant, William
Brickmakers
Bradbury, Thomas
Hampton, Enoch
Holmes & Clarke
Mills, George
Stonier, William
Ward, Henry

Britannia metal manufacturers

Britannia metal is an alloy of tin, antimony and copper and is similar to pewter.

Booth, Thomas
Dudson, James
Walklet, William H.

Brushmakers
Edwards, Edward
Johnson, Ambrose
Sherwin, Robert
Storey, Henry William

Builders
Jones, John (Mrs.)
Leonard, John
Matthews, Edward
Mellor, William
Ogden, James
Redfern, John
Steele, John
Wooldridge, Clement

Butchers
Allen, Lenford
Allsop, Josiah
Brook, John
Bull, John
Burton, Joseph
Carpmail, Moses
Chowner, John

Dutton, Frederick
Finney, John
Ford, William
Jones, William
Long, Henry
Massey, Emily (Mrs.)
Matthews, George
Mellor, Samuel
Riley, Thomas
Rushton, John
Sargeant, Thomas
Shipley, Edward
Shotton, Samuel
Simpson, Henry
Smith, George
Smith, Thomas
Sutton, William
Thorley, William
Turner, John
Warrillow, Anthony
Wooldridge, Edward

Butchers, Pork
Jones, Richard
Keates, Charles

Cabinet Makers
Nicklin, Lewis
Nicklin, Henry
Potts, Thomas
Potts, William
Sadler, Edward
Smith, Herbert
Wakefield, Thomas
Whittingham & Son

Camelhair Pencil Makers
Shelley, Sampson Astbury
Candle Makers
Kettle, William

Carpenters
Colclough, Samuel
Coxon, John
Ellis, George
Hammersley, Robert
Pope, Frederick

Carriage Proprietors
Swift, Henry

Cart Owners
Godwin, John

Carvers
Sutherland, Daniel

Cheese Factors
Walley, William Thomas
Warrington, John Thomas

Chemists
Brown, John
Brown, George
Evans, William Lawrence
Forrester, R. H.
Jones, Charles
Lloyd, John
Nicholls, Henry
Parkes, Ebenezer
Scarlett, William
Wilson, William
Wright, William
Yates, William Henry
Chemists & Druggists
Ellis, James
Booth, Richard

Chemists, Homopathic
Rowley, John Broadfield & Co.

Chimney Sweepers
Parkinson & Son

China Manufacturers
Wilkinson & Sons

China Figure Manufacturers
Dudson, James
Livesley, Powell & Co.
Worthington & Harrop

China Glass Dealers
Lawton, William

China Manufacturers
Allen, Herbert George
Baguley, George
Bevington, John
Brown, Westhead & Moore
Cooper, Thomas
Dudson, James

Ford, Thomas
Mills, Elizabeth (Mrs.)
Old Hall Earthenware Co.
Stubbs, William
Walley, John
Worthington & Green

China & Earthenware Mounters
Cosgrove & Martin
Walklet, William H.

China & Glass Dealers
Hastings, Mary Ann (Mrs.)

Clay merchants agents
Hollins, John

Clerks
Challinor, Edward

Clock & Watch Makers
Stevenson, John
Thomas, Joseph
Wyatt, Lewis

Clogmakers
Binns, George
Charlesworth, Richard
Fitton, Elizabeth (Mrs.)
Hilton, Joseph
Keys, Joseph
Leek, Thomas
Whitehead, William

Clothes Dealers
Palmer, Richard

Clothiers
Benjamin Solomon & Co.
Breveton, John
Fearn, George
Goodwin, George
Hammond, Alphonso
Harris & Co
Jesper, Samuel
Lazarus, Benjamin & Co.
Snook, Jonah
Steele, James
Swetman, John Hassall

Coach Builders
Cooper, Francis
Roycroft, Henry

Coal Dealers
Hawley, Richard
Holland, James
Hollowwood, John
Ryder, David
Shuttlebotham, James
Stubbs, Herbert
Taylor, George
Vigers, John

Coal Masters
Granville, Right Hon. Earl of

Coffee Room Proprietors
- see also Dining Room Proprietors
Howard, Joseph

Collieries
Baddeley, Richard
Heath, Robert
Shelton Colliery & Iron Works
Smith, Charles John
Yates, William

Colour Manufacturers
Adney, William
Boone, Alfred
Dodd, Thomas
Dudson, James
Goodwin, Joseph W.
Poulson, John
Stephenson, Joseph

Commercial Travellers
Painter, Frederick
Peake, John Machil
Bodley, Edward Fisher

Commission Agents
Foster, Henry
Narramore, Robert Edwin
Sergeant, George
Slaney, John

Confectioners
Aldersea, Sarah (Mrs.)
Alldridge, Charles

Allen, Ann (Mrs.)
Averill, Thomas
Berks, Henry
Evans, Henry
Hughes, Mary (Mrs.)
Kimberley, Thomas
Lamonby, Ann (Miss)
Robinson, William
Salt, Francis
Tristram, Josiah
Williams, Henry

Coopers
Pass, John
Rushton, Robert
Stanway, William
Wardle, George
Yellard, Almond

Corn & Flour Dealers
Downs, James
Edge & Barlow
Vigers, John

Cowkeepers
Lovett, Michael
Prince, William

Crate Makers
Davis, Elijah
Goodwin. Joseph
Heath, John
Hilton, Edward John
Hopwood, Joseph
Hopwood, William
Rushton, Robert
Salt, John
Sunnington, James
Walker, John

Curriers
Henstock, Thomas
Wallworth, James

Cutlers
Perry, Joseph
Shaw, George

Dairymen
Moseley, William Henry

Dealers
Mellor, Samuel
Decorative Painters
Hughes, John Alfred

Decorators
Buckley, John

Dentists
Crapper & Brierley

Designers
Chetwynd Brothers

Dining Room Proprietors
see also Coffee Room Proprietors
Buck, Ann (Mrs.)
Hulse, Robert
Johnson, William
Lloyd, Harriet (Mrs.)

Drapers
Poole, Richard
Robinson, James & Co.
Rushton, William
Stevenson, Josiah

Dressmakers
Bentley, Elizabeth (Mrs.),
Cadman,M. A. (Miss),
Clewlow, Sarah (Mrs.),
Cotton, Emily (Mrs.)
Dutton, Sarah (Miss)
Gill, Rosa (Miss)
Howlett, Emma (Mrs.)
Keeling, Ann (Miss)
Lawton, Alice (Miss)
Mellor, Margaret (Miss)
Robinson, Jane (Miss)
Stephenson, Naomi (Mrs.)

Drinks Manufacturers
Poitevin, Edward

Druggists
Leib, Paul Solomon
Lloyd, John
Pierce, Edward Lloyd
Scarlett, William

Dyers
Lewis, John Benjamin
Davies, John

Earthenware Manufacturers
Ashworth, George L.
Brown Westhead
Clementson, James
Dimmock, John & Co.
Dudson, James
Hood, George
Livesley Powell & Co.
Meakin, J. & G.
Old Hall Earthenware Co.
Oldham, James
Pankhurst & Co.
Ridgway, Edward John
Stubbs, William
Taylor, William
Taylor,Brothers & Co.
Twyford, Thomas
Unwin, Monntford & Taylor
Worthington & Son

Egg Dealers
Huston, Wilson
Wase, Esther (Mrs.)

Engineers
Warner, John
Engravers
Copeland, Thomas
Hordley, Thomas
Pepper, Elisha
Pope, William
Toft, Thomas

Estate Agents
Davis, Francis
Greaves, William

Fancy Repositories
Blundell, Catherine (Mrs.)
Hall, Jane (Miss)

Farmers
Woodward, Thomas

Farriers
Hodgkins, Samuel

Fishmongers
Bradbury, Samuel
Kelsall, Joseph
Rock, Thomas

Flint Grinders
Bowers, William
Brownfield, William
Clay, William & Co.
Keeling & Adams

Flint Merchants
Eastwood Mill Company

Flint Millers
Mycock & Son

Flour Dealers
Meek, Benjamin Brown

Fruit Dealers
Falkner, William

Fruit & Potato Merchants
Sutton, Charles

Fruiterers
Hood, Thomas
Massey, Josiah
Rowland, George
Simpson, Thomas
Stanton, John

Furniture Brokers
Litchfield, Henry
Miller, James
Pauley, William
Sidley, William

Gasfitters
Johnson, John
Davis, William

General Dealers
Boulton, Charles Bourne
Brammer, Ann (Mrs.)
McDonald, George
General Merchants
Mountford, Jno.
Wood & Son

Gilders
Evens, John
Sutherland, Daniel

Glass Dealers
Cole, Samuel & Co.
Leigh, Enoch

Granite Manufacturers
Taylor, William

Greengrocers
Barker, Elizabeth (Mrs.)
Bradbury, Thomas
Brunt, Jeremiah
Coxon, Elijah
Hawley, William
Haywood, James
McGrail, Patrick
Palin, Ann (Mrs.)
Snow, John
White, William

Grinders Of Potters' Materials
Eastwood Mill Company

Grocers
Adams, Boyce
Baker, John
Berks, William
Bradbury, William
Broadhurst, James & George
Brown, Thomas
Collett, Bernard
Cooper, John
Docksey, John
Edge, John
Ellis, Henry
Ellis, Richard
Freeman, William
Gilman, Thomas
Grosvenor, Edward
Hackney, Cordelia (Mrs.)
Harrison, Charles
Hewitt, William
Hollins, John
James, William
Kenway, Luscombe & Co.
Lawton, William Wright
Lees, Ralph

Lyons, Isaac
Mayer, Joseph
Miller, John
Moore, Edward Thomas
Platt, John Spalton
Richardson, Isaac
Ridgway, George
Ridgway & Foulkes
Salmon, James
Shaw, Richard
Sherratt, Hugh Hulme
Shuttlebotham, John
Spencer, Henry
Streete, Henry John
Vigers, John
Walley, Mary (Mrs.)
Wells, George
Wright, Joseph

Gunpowder Agents
Glover, Arthur

Gunsmiths
Hickin, William

Haberdashers
Clifford & Griffiths
Lawton, Thomas
Turner, Edward

Hairdressers
Bates, Joseph
Beech, Henry
Berks, Charles
Billington, Richard
Dark, Richard Morgan
Finney, Joseph F.
Finney, Francis
Haslehurst, George
Moreton, Ralph
Picken, James
Salmons, Thomas
Simpson, Robert
Walthall, William
Wedgwood, John
Wilkinson, Edwin

Hatters
Boyd, John
Cade, William

Cartlidge, George
Griffiths, George B.
Hibbert, William

Hay & Straw Dealers
Dale, Josiah
Peake, Joseph
Simpson, George

Herbalists
Taylor, James

Hop & Malt Merchants
Adams, Thomas

Hosiers
Barker, William
Buxton, Ann (Mrs.)
Carr, Hannah (Mrs.)
Clifford & Griffiths
Foulkes, Mary (Mrs.)
Gee, John
Guildford, Reuben
Harris, Mary (Mrs.)
Joynson, William
Sands,Thomas
Tittensor, George
Walklet, Henry William
Innkeepers
Anderson, William
Barlow, William Henry
Beardmore, Theophilus
Berry, William
Biddulph, William
Birch, Charles
Blagg, Henry
Boden, John
Brierley, Mary (Mrs.)
Carr, Peter
Cheadle, J. C.
Clewes, William, jun.
Colclough, John
Colclough, Isaac
Copeland, John
Dale, George
Davis, Thomas
Dickens, Perrey
Draycott, Thomas
Edwards, Richard
Edwards, William

Hosiers - contd
Farr, Thomas
Forrester, David
Fradley, Solomon
Hall, Roger
Hambleton, William
Hampton, Enoch
Hancock, John
Harlow, Rebecca (Mrs.)
Huston, William
Jaques, Samuel
Lunt, Samuel
Meigh, John Aynsley
Morris, John
Palin, James
Palmer, Thomas
Penney, Harriet (Mrs.)
Platt, Henry
Rigby, Samuel
Rowley, Bagnall
Sawyer, James
Schofield, Robert
Slater, Thomas
Smith, John Henry
Stubbs, Christopher
Swift, Henry
Turner, Charles
Twyford, Christopher
Wheeler, Martin
Wilkinson, John
Wood, George
Wooldridge, Richard
Worthington, Samuel
Wright, Benjamin

Iron Masters
Granville, Rt. Hon. Earl of
Smith, Charles John

Ironfounders
Gibson & Evans
Harris, William Dean
Jackson, Edward
Langley, Richard J.
Pidduck, Thomas
Spencer, John

Ironstone China Manufacturers
Ironstone china, a mixture of white clay, slag from iron smelting and pulverised flint, was patented by the London china dealer, Miles Mason. It was an inexpensive substitute for bone china and was very popular in England and America in the nineteenth century.

Ashworth, George L.
Dudson, James

Ironworks
Bull, Joseph
Shelton Bar Iron Co.
Shelton Colliery Iron Wks

Jasper Makers
Jasper is a crystalline form of silica and is used for ornamentation or as gemstones.

Venables, Henry

Jewellers
Pidduck, Henry
Rivers, William Mollart

Joiners
Boothroyd, Emmerson
Eggington, Horatio
Gleeson, William
Hordley, Thomas
Land Surveyors
Homer, Charles James Horatio

Lead Merchants
Taylor, William

Leather Merchants and Sellers
Broughton, Samuel
Godwin, John
Henstock, Thomas

Libraries
Pottery Mechanics' Institution
Statham, George Leveridge

Licensees to Let Horses
Marshall, Robert

Linendrapers

Acres, Thomas P.
Boulton, John & Son
Bourne, Samuel
Bradford, George
Clifford & Griffiths
Davenport, Uriah
Dean, Elizabeth (Mrs.)
Glover, James
Huntbach, Michael
Marsden & Son
Ringland, Hans
Swift, Thomas

Majolica Manufacturers

Majolica is a form of earthenware with colourful lead glazes and molded surfaces. First produced by Mintons Ltd at the Great Exhibition of 1851 it was in the style of the Italian maiolica ware with which it is often confused.

Bailey Murrells & Co.

Manufacturers of Water Closet Pans

Buckley, John

Manufacturing Chemists

Booth, William Ward

Marine Store Dealers

Brockley, George
Forrester, Joseph
Gee, John
Wray, Joseph

Market Superintendents

Butterworth, John

Marl Manufacturers

Mills, George

Mattress Makers

Beddall, John

Merchants

Bradshaw, John
Kenway, Luscombe & Co.
Miller
Buckley, John

Milliners

Adams, Charlotte
Barcroft, Susan
Beddow, Emma
Brooksby, Agnes
Brough, Ann
Browne, Samuel
Cadman, M. A.
Cartwright, Ann
Colclough, Hannah
Dean, Ann
Edwards, Sarah
Emery, Susan & Fanny
Foster, Ann
France, Mary Ann
Gould, Phoebe
Jones, Louisa & Rose
McDonald, Isabella
Nicklin, Sarah Ann
Pointon, Martha
Riles, Eliza
Robinson, Jane
Rushton, William
Salmon, Eliza
Sedgley, Eliza
Simpson, Kitty Maria
Stanway, Amy
Stephenson, Naomi
Thorley, Elizabeth
Ward, Louise

Mining Engineers & Surveyors

Maddock, Thomas

Modellers

Chetwynd Brothers
Walker, James

Nail Makers

Bates, William
Fletcher, Ellen

Newsagents

Craddock, William
Johnson, Elijah
Mitchell, Stephen
Rigby, John
Smith, William
Wilbraham, Thomas

Newspapers
Staffordshire Advertiser
Staffordshire Sentinel

Nursermen & Seedsman
Cartlidge, Theophilus

Painters
Lunt, Samuel
Scarratt, George
Smith, George

Paper Makers
Brittain, Thomas & Son

Paperhanging Warehouses
Goodwin, William
Whittingham & Son

Parian Manufacturers
Parian Ware was an inexpensive substitute for marble and fashionable in Victorian England.

Bailey Murrells & Co.
Evens, John
Livesley, Powell & Co.
Roe, Henry & Son
Salt, Charles
Smith, John
Stanway & Horne
Stubbs, William
Walley, John
Wardle & Ash
Warrington, William & Co.
Wilkinson & Sons

Patent Cock Spur & Still Manufacturers
Buller (Wentworth William) & Mugford

Pattern Manufacturers
Binns, George

Pawnbrokers
Butters, Charles
Hammersley, John
Hill & Cooke
Steele & Machin
Swetman, John Hassall
Vessey, Thomas Watson

Photographers
Chester, Stephen
Emery, John
Spilsbury, William

Pianoforte & Music Sellers
Emery, John jun.
Whittingham, John Fowler

Pin Manufacturers
Ford, Charles

Plumbers
Billington, James
Birchall, Robert
Forrester, William
Goldstraw, Samuel
Heath, Abraham & Charles
Lunt, Samuel
Scarratt, George
Scarratt, Joseph
Scarratt & Bickley
Sedgley, William
Woolliscroft & Penton

Porcelain Manufacturers
Bevington, Samuel
Livesley, Powell & Co.
Wilkinson & Sons
The Enamel Porcelain Co. Ltd

Portrait Painters
Emery, John

Posting Houses
Swift, Henry (Saracen's Head)
Turner, Charles (King's Head)

Potters' Material Dealers
Boddington, William c.

Potters' Tool Makers
Fenton, Samuel
Leak, Eliza (Mrs.)
Leak, Leveson

Pottery Manufacturers
Harding, William & Joseph

Printers

Adams, Henry
James, John
Potter & Ford
Sheardown & Daniel
Staffordshire Advertiser
Staffordshire Sentinel

Provision Dealers

Broster, Ann (Mrs.)
Cope, Thomas
Hollins, John
Kent, George
Rochell, Hannah (Mrs.)
Shaw, Richard
Stranaghan, Elizabeth (Mrs)
Stranaghan, James

Railway Companies

Staffordshire Potteries Street Railway

Religious Tract Depots

Wright, Susan (Miss)

Reporters

Cherry, John Law

Rustic Ware Makers

Baddeley, James

Saddlers

Allcock, Ralph
Beech, Robert
Croston, William
Eardley, Thomas

Sausage Makers

Keates, Charles

Saw Makers

Kenyon, Thomas

Saw Mills

Palmer, Henry
Schools, Academies, Teachers Etc.
Alfieri, Charles
Chantrey, Thomas
Davies, Evan
Goodwin, Ellen (Miss)
Heath, Ann Mare (Miss)
Iddins, John

Malkin, Elijah
Mellor, Thomas
Osmond, Charles Marsh
Sedgley, Mary (Miss)
Tourton, Claudius
Whittingham, John Fowler

Schools, Academies, Teachers Etc.

Alfieri, Charles
Chantrey, Thomas
Davies, Evan
Goodwin, Ellen (Miss)
Heath, Ann Mare (Miss)
Iddins, John
Johnson, Catherine (Miss)
Malkin, Elijah
Mellor, Thomas
Osmond, Charles Marsh
Sedgley, Mary (Miss)
Tourton, Claudius
Whittingham, John Fowler

Secretaries

Cartledge, Henry
Hassell, William

Shopkeepers

Allen, John
Austin, Harriet (Mrs.)
Bagnall, John
Barlow, James
Beddow, Martha & Eleanor
Beech, Mary (Mrs.)
Bentley, Marinda (Mrs.)
Berrisford, John
Birkin, Bryan
Boughey, William
Boulton, Eliza (Mrs.)
Brindley, Lucy (Mrs.)
Brown, James
Capewell, Edward
Castellow, Michael
Charlesworth, Richard
Conway, Edward
Cooper, William
Coulter, Margaret Ann
Coxon, John
Curzon, Samuel
Dean, Frederick
Devonport, James

Shopkeepers - contd.

Dunn, Thomas
Ellis, Hannah (Mrs.)
Emery, Lewis
Foulkes, Anne (Mrs.)
Fox, Joseph
Gater, Thomas
Gibson, Elizabeth (Mrs.)
Giles, Joseph
Greaves, John
Green, Herbert
Griffiths, John
Hall, John
Hammersley, Sarah (Mrs.)
Harrington, William
Hawley, John
Hickin, Henry
Hodkinson, Martha (Mrs.)
Hopkinson, Frederick
Howlett, John
Johnson, Richard
Jones, Robert
Keeling, James
Keen, Mark
Key, Josiah
Lakin, Thomas
Lawton, Martha (Mrs.)
Leader, Matthew
Lightfoot, Elijah
Lomas, William
Lomas, George
Massey, William Henry
Massey, Mary (Mrs.)
Meigh, George
Mountford, Samuel
Nicholls, Henry
Owens, Edward
Parton, Henry
Paton, John
Peake, Samuel
Pedley, James
Pembleton, Sarah (Mrs.)
Perry, John
Perry, Hannah (Mrs.)
Pickering, Henry
Plant, Henry
Pointon, Aaron
Poole, Sarah (Mrs.)
Poole, Hamlet

Presbury, William
Ratcliff, George
Redfern, John Ellis
Ridgway, Thomas
Roberts, Daniel
Roberts, John
Robinson, James
Rowley, John
Sargeant, Charles
Sheldon, James
Sherwin, Henry
Shipley, Thomas
Shirley, William
Simpson, Elizabeth (Mrs.)
Smith, John
Smith, Edward
Smytheman, William
Sneyd, James
Stanley, John
Steele, William
Taylor, Thomas
Thompson,. Henry
Shopkeepers - contd.
Thorpe, Thomas
Till, John
Till & Brown
Twigg, George
Walker, William
Walley, Noah
Walley, Titus
Warrington, William
Williams, David
Wilson, Edward
Woodward, John
Wright, William
Wright, John
Yates, Samuel

Silk Lawn Manufacturers
Coates & Co.

Silk Mercers
Clifford & Griffiths

Skin Dealers
Rowley & Co.

Smallware Dealers
Quoroll, John

Smalt Manufacturers

Smalt is a deep blue coloured powdered glass.

Meigh, William Mellor

Societies and Institutes

Hepworth & Co.
New Mechanics' Institute
North Staffordshire Guardian Society for the Protection of Trade
North Staffordshire Museum
Potteries & Newcastle loan society
Pottery Mechanics' Institution
Staffordshire Potteries Loan Society

Solicitors

Amos, Samuel
Bishop & Blakiston
Brown, Hugh
Challinor, Edward
Moxon, James
Paddock, George jun
Stevenson, Ralph
Tennant, Edmund

Spirit Merchants

Dix, Alexander Mills
Worthington, Samuel

Stationers

Bebbington, James
Redfern, Mary (Mrs.)

Staymakers

Roden, Jane (Miss)
Stonemasons
Clewes, Jesse
Hunt, George

Stoneware Manufacturers

Johnson, William
Stanway & Horne

Stoneware Manufacturers

Stubbs, William
Straw Bonnet Makers
Andrew, Mary (Mrs.)
Howlett, Sarah (Miss)
Mountford, Mary (Mrs.)

Parr & Taylor (Misses)
Stanway, Amy (Mrs.)
Taylor, Ann (Mrs.)
Taylor, Elizabeth (Miss)

Surgeons

Boothroyd, Benjamin
Davis, Joseph Barnard
Davis, William Haslam
Fairmann, John Bertram
Folker, William Henry
Garner, Robert
Girdlestone, Horatio
Grosvenor, William
McBean, Alexander
Moore, George Lennox
Scott, Henry
Walker, John Swift

Surveyors

Forbes, Joseph Samuel
Scrivener, Robert
Shaw, Thomas Cotterill
Stevens & Forbes

Tailors

Akers, Edward
Barrett, William
Bednall, Joseph
Bell, John
Berrisford, George
Boult, Charles
Brooksby, Henry
Buckley, James
Gilman, Thomas & Robert
Harrison, William
Lucas, Alfred
Meredith, John
Nixon, Henry
Radford, John
Silvester, William
Smith, Theophilus
Spencer, John
Stokes, Thomas
Wallace, James
Williams, David
Woolley, Thomas

Tallow Chandlers

Kenway, Luscombe & Co.

Tea Dealers
Irwin, Thomas
Kenway, Luscombe & Co.
Lloyd, John
Mountford, Prudence (Mrs.)
Platt, John Spalton
Vigers, John

Timber Merchants
Nicholls, T. & R.

Tinplate Workers
Brougham, William
Dickin, Charles
Fosbrook, Peter James
Johnson, James
Lacy, Rose (Mrs.)
Lyons, Martin

Tobacco Manufacturers
Smith & Keen

Tobacco Pipe Makers
Gray, Robert Henry

Tobacconists
Brown, Samuel
Farrell, Eliza (Mrs.)
Sutton, Elizabeth (Miss)
Toussaint, Edward & Co.
Woolliscroft, William

Toy Dealers
Winfield, John

Trunk Makers
Berrisford, Benjamin

Turncocks
Espley, George
Harding, Richard

Umbrella Makers
Robson, Henry

Undertakers
Clifford & Griffiths

Upholsterers
Whittingham & Son

Veterinary Surgeons
Baddeley, Wm. Warburton

Warehouses
Greencamun, Thoms
Henstock, Thomas

Watch & Clock Makers
Bradley, Joseph
Dutton, Abraham
Pidduck, Henry
Rivers, William Mollart
Toft, Thomas
Welch, John

Wheelwrights
Brooks, Ralph
Capper, Joseph
Hand, Charles
Horne, Thomas
Mellor, Thomas

Whip Dealers
Dixon, John
Wine & Spirit Merchants
Baker, John & George
Farr, Thomas
Hall, William
Swift, Henry
Turner, Charles

Wire Workers
Nunns, James

Wood Turners
Smith & Sons
Till, Rupert

Hanley in 1864

From page 26

William Brownfield, Esq., of Chatterley House, ex-mayor, contributes the sum of £650 to found a working-men's reading room, forming a portion of the erection; the designs are by Mr. Scrivener, architect. A cemetery was consecrated, April 30th, 1860, by the lord bishop of the diocese. There are a subscription library, public news room, and a theatre.

The Town Hall is an elegant and spacious stone building, erected at a cost of £4,500. The County Court for the district is held in the Town Hall monthly; the district includes the following places: Burslem, Tunstall and Hanley; and petty sessions are held every Monday and alternate Thursday; Thomas Bailey Rose, Esq., the stipendiary magistrate for the district, presiding over the former, and the mayor and borough magistrates over the latter. The Police Office is also at the Town Hall.

The North Staffordshire Infirmary is a large building, situated on an open and elevated position in the Shelton liberty.

There are three excellent spacious covered markets for meat, fish, and vegetables: Wednesday and Saturday (the latter the principal) are the market days; a cattle market is held every Tuesday, and is now of considerable importance. Martinmas (November 11th) is the annual hiring time for the potters. The great festivals of the district are the Stoke Wakes, which commence the first Sunday in August. The Pottery Central Savings Bank was established in 1823.

The town owes its prosperity to the extensive china and earthenware manufactories. One of the largest in the Potteries has just been completed from the plan of Mr. Scrivener, architect; it forms one immense range of brick building, the property of Messrs. John Dimmock and Co. The mines of coal and ironstone which abound in the neighbourhood also contribute to the local economy. A large portion of the mines belongs to the Duchy of Lancaster, of which Earl Granville is the lessee, by whom extensive ironworks and collieries are here carried on. A copyhold court under the Duchy is held monthly at the Town Hall, at which John Ward, Esq., the deputy registrar, presides.- The Queen is the lady of the manor.

www.ingramcontent.com/pod-product-compliance
Lightning Source LLC
Chambersburg PA
CBHW070233290526
45789CB00004B/1607